The *Poet* and the *Professor*

Grade **4**

Poems for Building Reading Skills

Stuck

If I could be a famous star, a famous movie queen,
the world would watch me acting on the giant silver screen!
I'd have half a dozen houses. I'd have twenty-seven cars.
I'd have twice as many loyal fans as all the other stars.

If I could be an astronaut, a rocket-riding ace,
I'd put a shiny spacesuit on and soar out into space.
I'd flutter like a feather. I'd float like a balloon.
I'd fly a girl-manned missile, and I'd land it on the moon.

Oh, all the things I'd love to do, it's such a lovely dream;
but I'm stuck here in this classroom, and it makes me want to scream.

Authors

Brod Bagert and Timothy Rasinski

Contributing Author

Kathleen Knoblock

SHELL EDUCATION

Publishing Credits

Dona Herweck Rice, *Editor-in-Chief*; Lee Aucoin, *Creative Director*; Don Tran, *Print Production Manager*; Conni Medina, M.S.Ed., *Editorial Director*; Tamara Hollingsworth, *Editor*; Jodene Lynn Smith, *Editor*; Evelyn Garcia, *Assistant Editor*; Robin Erickson, *Interior Layout Designer*; Neri Garcia, *Production Artist*; Stephanie Reid, *Production Artist*; Corinne Burton, M.S.Ed., *Publisher*

Letters and Poems © Brod Bagert 2010

McREL Standards © 2004 www.mcrel.org/standards-benchmarks

All recordings performed by Brod Bagert. Recorded, edited, and mastered by Ross Ricks at Surf City Sound. www.surfcitysound.com

Shell Education

5301 Oceanus Drive
Huntington Beach, CA 92649-1030
http://www.shelleducation.com
ISBN 978-1-4258-0238-7
© 2010 Shell Educational Publishing, Inc.
Reprinted 2012

Table of Contents

Research

Developing students' reading skills is a critical goal that begins in the primary grades. Yet with each successive grade, students must acquire increasing skills at reading and understanding a variety of texts. *The Poet and the Professor: Poems for Building Reading Skills* provides valuable instructional tools and engaging materials and activities for increasing student skills in reading, writing, listening, and speaking. As you use the poems, lessons, and activities in this book, you will know that you are not only providing instruction based on solid educational research, but also giving students opportunities to learn and practice specific academic standards.

The Poet and the Professor: Poems for Building Reading Skills has been designed to provide high-interest instructional texts and lessons based on best practices in reading education. The concept of the book was developed by Dr. Timothy Rasinski, Professor of Literacy Education at Kent State University and author of numerous articles, books, and publications on reading education. The poems in this book were written by Brod Bagert, whose catchy and humorous books of poetry have entertained and inspired scores of young people to embrace poetry.

In its *Report of the National Reading Panel: Teaching Children to Read* (2006), the National Reading Panel noted predominant themes in the research on the development of reading comprehension skills. The core of *The Poet and the Professor: Poems for Building Reading Skills* revolves around the NRP's findings, specifically, 1) "Reading comprehension is a complex cognitive process that cannot be understood without a clear description of the role that vocabulary development and vocabulary instruction play in the understanding of what has been read,"

and 2) "Comprehension is an active process that requires an intentional and thoughtful interaction between the reader and the text."

Making Connections

Studies show that making connections—drawing upon prior knowledge, emotions, opinions, understandings, and experiences—helps students better understand what they are reading (Harvey and Goudvis 2000). Keene and Zimmermann (1997) concluded that students comprehend better when they make different kinds of connections: text-to-self, text-to-text, and text-to-world.

Text-to-self connections are those that are individual and personal. For example, in Lesson 7 of this book, prior to reading a poem about a student who feels empowered when he plays video games, the Making Connections section suggests having students think about something that they are especially good at and how it makes them feel when they do it.

Text-to-text connections are those that identify similarities between one thing that has been read (whether a whole book or a single word) and a new text. In other words, students use the familiar to help them understand the unfamiliar.

Text-to-world connections are those that are more global than personal. These include information or impressions students have acquired from such things as reading stories and watching movies (narrative), studying science or social studies (expository), seeing ads on TV or in magazines (persuasive), and participating in discussions. One goal of this book is to challenge students to draw upon their prior knowledge and experiences to prepare them to better understand what they will read.

Comprehension Strategies

Comprehension is defined as "intentional thinking during which meaning is constructed through interactions between text and reader" (Harris and Hodges 1995). In its findings, the National Reading Panel (2006) states that "the rationale for the explicit teaching of comprehension skills is that comprehension can be improved by teaching students to use specific cognitive strategies or to reason strategically when they encounter barriers to understanding what they are reading." The panel further notes that "explicit or formal instruction in the application of comprehension strategies has been shown to be highly effective in enhancing understanding."

Effective reading instruction, then, must include teaching students strategies that they can employ as they read in order to increase comprehension. Hosenfeld (1993) states that expert readers freely and appropriately use a variety of strategies to gain understanding as they read. There are many effective strategies, including predicting, rephrasing, asking and answering questions (Bottomley and Osborn 1993) and using graphic organizers (Jensen 1998). Teaching and modeling reading comprehension strategies through structured and explicit instruction will enable students to learn how to comprehend text (Rosenshine and Meister 1994). The result of both explicit teaching and modeling is that students are learning when and how to use these strategies to construct meaning (Carter 1997).

Within the lessons of *The Poet and the Professor: Poems for Building Reading Skills*, numerous comprehension strategies are presented and explained, and students are given opportunities to apply these strategies. Each lesson focuses on a single strategy, but all lessons are in whole-group format, so students may learn from one another as well as from the teacher.

The goal of teaching a variety of comprehension strategies is to give students a cache of tools to call upon when interacting with any text. As students move from reading words to reading ideas, concepts, and information, they learn to use these tools more and more effectively. In essence, comprehension tools enable students to not just read what someone wrote but also to read what someone communicated.

Standards-Based Skills

In many states, teachers are required to demonstrate how their lessons meet state standards. Standards are statements that describe the knowledge, skills, and content students should acquire at each level. Standards are also used to develop standardized tests to evaluate students' academic progress.

Each lesson in *The Poet and the Professor: Poems for Building Reading Skills* is correlated to language arts standards for grades 3–5. See the correlation chart on pages 13–14 for the skills covered in this book.

Each Standards-Based Skill Focus section of the lesson plan page highlights a specific benchmark skill needed to achieve the overall standard. As you teach the standards-based skills in this book, you can be assured that they have been identified as appropriate for students in grades 3–5.

Vocabulary Word Study

The National Reading Panel (2006) recognizes the importance of vocabulary knowledge in the development of reading skills. After examining over 20,000 research citations, the panel concluded that studies suggest that "vocabulary instruction does lead to gains in comprehension," and that "vocabulary should be taught both directly and indirectly." The panel specifically mentions that "repetition and multiple exposures to vocabulary items are important" and that "learning in rich contexts enhances the acquisition of vocabulary."

Word knowledge and reading comprehension go hand in hand. In fact, "vocabulary knowledge is one of the best predictors of reading achievement" (Richek 2005). Further, "vocabulary knowledge promotes reading fluency, boosts reading comprehension, improves academic achievement, and enhances thinking and communication" (Bromley 2004). Vocabulary also assists in reading comprehension. Noted reading scholar and researcher Michael Pressley (2001) states that vocabulary instruction has direct effects on reading comprehension. Students who understand the words they read are more likely to comprehend what they have read.

The Poet and the Professor: Poems for Building Reading Skills reflects the practices found to be effective by many researchers. These include:

- teaching vocabulary in a word-rich context
- teaching selected words intentionally while encouraging unintentional acquisition as well
- providing multiple types of information about words
- guiding students to make connections between known and unknown words
- using strategies that increase students' ability to learn new words on their own

For example, one strategy for learning new words is clarifying, as seen in Lesson 7. After finding targeted vocabulary words in the poem, the Vocabulary Word Study section suggests that students clarify the meanings by answering questions such as, "Is a *cheetah* a type of cat or a type of cracker? Which means the same as *capture*—release or catch? Would you want to *conquer* an enemy or a friend?"

Differentiation

Classrooms have evolved into diverse pools of learners with gifted children, English language learners, high achievers, learning-disabled children, underachievers, and average achievers. Teachers are expected to meet their diverse needs in one classroom. Differentiation encompasses what is taught, how it is taught, and the products children create to show what they have learned. These categories are often referred to as content, process, and product:

- Differentiating by content means putting more depth into the curriculum by organizing the curriculum concepts and structure of knowledge.
- Differentiating by process requires the use of varied instructional techniques and materials to enhance learning.
- Differentiating by product means that children are asked to show their learning in ways that will enhance their cognitive development and personal expression.

Teachers can keep these categories in mind as they plan instruction that will best meet the needs of their students.

Differentiating for Below-Grade-Level Students

Below-grade-level students will probably need concepts to be made more concrete for them. They may also need extra guidance in developing oral and written language. By receiving extra support and understanding, these students will feel more secure and have greater success. Suggested ideas include:

- Allow partner work for instructional activities.
- Allocate extra practice time.
- Allow for kinesthetic (hands-on) activities where appropriate.

Differentiating for Above-Grade-Level Students

These students usually learn concepts very quickly. The activities and end products can be adapted to be appropriate for individual students. Suggested ideas include:

- Assign students the activities that represent more complex concepts.
- Assign more complex oral and written responses.
- Have students design their own learning strategies and share them with the class.

Differentiating for English Language Learners

English language learners make up an ever-increasing percentage of our school-age population. Like all students, English language learners need teachers who have a strong knowledge base and commitment to developing students' language. It is crucial that teachers work carefully to develop English language learners' academic vocabularies. Teachers should keep in mind the following important practices:

- Create a comfortable atmosphere that encourages students to use language.
- Respect and draw on students' backgrounds and experiences and build connections between the known and the new.
- Model and scaffold language use.
- Make use of realia, concrete materials, visuals, pantomime, and other nonlinguistic representations of concepts to make input comprehensible. Write new words on the board as they are shared or provide each student with a set of cards that contain the words.
- Provide wait time to allow students time to put their thoughts into words.

Differentiating by Proficiency Levels for English Language Learners

All teachers should know the levels of language acquisition for each of their English language learners. Knowing these levels will help to plan instruction. (The category titles vary from district to district or state to state, but the general descriptions are common.) Students at level 1 will need a lot of language support in all the activities. Using visuals to support oral and written language will help to make the language more comprehensible. These students "often understand much more than they are able to express" (Herrell and Jordan 2004). It is the teacher's job to move them from listening to language to expressing language. Students at levels 2 and 3 will benefit from pair work in speaking tasks, but they will need additional individual support during writing and reading tasks. Students at levels 4 and 5 (or 6, in some cases) may appear to be fully proficient in the English language. However, because they are English language learners, they may still struggle with comprehending the academic language used during instruction. They may also struggle with reading and writing.

The following chart shows the proficiency levels at a quick glance. The levels are based on the World-Class Instructional Design and Assessment (WIDA) Consortium (WIDA 2007).

Proficiency Levels at a Quick Glance

Proficiency Level	Questions to Ask	Activities/Actions		
Level 1—Entering minimal comprehension no verbal production	Where is…? What examples do you see? What are the parts of…?	listen	draw	mime
		point	circle	respond (one or two words)
Level 2—Beginning limited comprehension short spoken phrases	Can you list three…? What facts or ideas show…? What do the facts mean?	move	select	act/act out
		match	choose	list
Level 3—Developing increased comprehension simple sentences	How did ____ happen? Why do you think…? If you could __, what would you do?	name	list	respond (phrases or sentences)
		label	categorize	tell/say
Level 4—Expanding very good comprehension some errors in speech	How would you show…? What would result if…? Why is this important?	recall	retell	define
		compare/ contrast	explain	summarize
		describe	role-play	restate
Level 5—Bridging comprehension comparable to native-English speakers speaks using complex sentences	What is meant by…? What is an original way to show…? Why is it better that…?	analyze	defend	complete
		evaluation	justify	support
		create	describe	express

How to Use This Book

The Poet and the Professor: Poems for Building Reading Skills is a succession of lessons built around a compilation of poems. The program includes the book (which is a teacher's resource for using the poems to build reading skills), the Audio CD, and the Teacher Resource CD.

This book contains the 30 letters and poems used in the program. Accompanying each letter or poem is a lesson plan that contains the sections Making Connections, Comprehension Strategy, Standards-Based Skill Focus, and Vocabulary Word Study. Information and ideas about how to relate the poem to each of these areas is provided on this page. For more information about each section, see the Research section of the book (pp. 4–6). In addition, two activity pages are provided that relate to the Standards-Based Skill Focus and the Vocabulary Word Study sections of the lesson plan.

The Audio CD contains recordings of each of the letters and poems in the book. Students can follow the text on their own copies of the poem pages, on an interactive whiteboard, or on an overhead projector.

The Teacher Resource CD contains a variety of resources that can be used to enhance the lessons provided in this book. The color poem can be photocopied on a transparency, displayed on an interactive whiteboard, or printed and copied for each student. The color activity pages are included on the Teacher Resource CD as well as a page-turning book that includes all of the letters and poems used in this program. This page-turning book allows students to refer to all the poems in a digital format. This page-turning book can also be displayed on an interactive whiteboard for easy viewing during a whole-class lesson.

The Poet and the Professor: Poems for Building Reading Skills has been designed to supplement any reading/language arts program. The following is a suggested routine for incorporating the poetry, reading comprehension, skills, and word study activities into your weekly lessons.

Day	Suggested Instructional Plan
Day 1	Before sharing the poem with students, prepare them for reading with the suggested discussion and activities in the Making Connections section of the lesson. Conclude by modeling fluent reading of the poem.
Day 2	Display the poem and/or provide a copy of the poem for each student. Begin by rereading the poem, modeling proper tone, expression, and pace. Encourage students to follow along as you read. Next, use the suggestions in the Comprehension Strategy section for whole-group teaching and discussion. Allow students to refer to the poem as they explore the strategies for understanding its literal and interpretive meaning. Day 2 would also be a good time to reread the poem several times, incorporating various fluency-building techniques. Suggested techniques include: • read-and-repeat (also known as echo reading, refrain reading, or call and response) • paired reading • choral reading (in a whole group or small groups, or as line-a-child) • reader's theater (performance reading) For detailed information about these techniques and more, see Rasinski (2003) in the References Cited section on page 143 of this book.
Day 3	Use Day 3 to concentrate on skill development. Begin with the suggested activities in the Standards-Based Skill Focus section of the lesson. Then give students the opportunity to apply the skill by completing the reproducible activity sheet that corresponds with the lesson.

How to Use This Book (cont.)

Day	Suggested Instructional Plan
Day 4	Focus on vocabulary and word study. Begin with the activities suggested in the Vocabulary Word Study section of the lesson. Then reinforce the words and concepts introduced by having students complete the corresponding reproducible activity sheet. At the end of each Word Study page is an optional extension activity. You may use this as homework, as extra credit, or as a regular writing assignment to be done in class the following day.
Day 5	Choose one or more of the following suggested activities to wrap up the week's lesson: • Have students complete the extension activity from the Word Study page. • Take a few minutes of class time to review together the skill and word study pages students completed in this week's lesson. • Allow students to practice, and then perform the poem for one another, you, or another class. • Have students keep a journal in which they write to respond to each poem at the conclusion of the lesson. • Provide students with (or have them select on their own) words from the poem to practice alphabetizing, to write their own sentences or poems, to create word puzzles or word maps/ladders, or to create their own poems.

Standards Correlations

Shell Education is committed to producing educational materials that are research and standards based. In this effort, we have correlated all of our products to the academic standards of all 50 states, the District of Columbia, and the Department of Defense Dependent Schools.

How to Find Standards Correlations

To print a customized correlation report of this product for your state, visit our website at **http://www.shelleducation.com** and follow the on-screen directions. If you require assistance in printing correlation reports, please contact Customer Service at 1-877-777-3450.

Purpose and Intent of Standards

The No Child Left Behind legislation mandates that all states adopt academic standards that identify the skills students will learn in kindergarten through grade twelve. While many states had already adopted academic standards prior to NCLB, the legislation set requirements to ensure the standards were detailed and comprehensive.

Standards are designed to focus instruction and guide adoption of curricula. Standards are statements that describe the criteria necessary for students to meet specific academic goals. They define the knowledge, skills, and content students should acquire at each level. Standards are also used to develop standardized tests to evaluate students' academic progress.

Teachers are required to demonstrate how their lessons meet state standards. State standards are used in development of all of our products, so educators can be assured they meet the academic requirements of each state.

McREL Compendium

We use the Mid-continent Research for Education and Learning (McREL) Compendium to create standards correlations. Each year, McREL analyzes state standards and revises the compendium. By following this procedure, McREL is able to produce a general compilation of national standards. Each lesson in this product is based on one or more McREL standards. The chart on the following pages lists each standard taught in this product and the page number(s) for the corresponding lesson(s).

Standards Correlation Chart

The chart below correlates the activities in *The Poet and the Professor: Poems for Building Reading Skills* with the McREL Content Knowledge.

Standards for Language Arts Grades 3–5

Standards	Benchmarks	Lesson
Uses listening and speaking strategies for different purposes	8.1 Contributes to group discussions	All
	8.3 Responds to questions and comments (e.g., gives reasons in support of opinion, responds to others' ideas)	All
	8.4 Listens to classmates and adults (e.g., does not interrupt, faces the speaker, asks questions, summarizes or paraphrases to confirm understanding, gives feedback, eliminates barriers to effective listening)	All
	8.6 Uses level-appropriate vocabulary in speech (e.g., familiar idioms, similes, word play)	13
	8.9 Uses a variety of verbal communication skills	14, 20
Uses general skills and strategies of the reading process	5.1 Previews text (e.g., skims material; uses pictures, textual clues, and text format)	All
	5.3 Makes, confirms, and revises simple predictions about what will be found in a text (e.g., uses prior knowledge and ideas presented in text, illustrations, titles, topic sentences, key words, and foreshadowing clues)	All
	5.4 Uses phonetic and structural analysis techniques, syntactic structure, and semantic context to decode unknown words (e.g., vowel patterns, complex word families, syllabication, root words, affixes)	6
	5.7 Understands level-appropriate reading vocabulary (e.g., synonyms, antonyms, homophones, multi-meaning words)	12, 22
	5.8 Monitors own reading strategies and makes modifications as needed (e.g., recognizes when he or she is confused by a section of text, questions whether the text makes sense)	30
	5.10 Understands the author's purpose (e.g., to persuade, to inform) or point of view	30
Uses reading skills and strategies to understand and interpret a variety of literary texts	6.1 Uses reading skills and strategies to understand a variety of literary passages and texts (e.g., fairy tales, folktales, fiction, nonfiction, myths, poems, fables, fantasies, historical fiction, biographies, autobiographies, chapter books)	All
	6.5 Understands elements of character development in literary works (e.g., differences between main and minor characters; stereotypical characters as opposed to fully developed characters; changes that characters undergo; the importance of a character's actions, motives, and appearance to plot and theme)	2, 30
	6.7 Understands the ways in which language is used in literary texts (e.g., personification, alliteration, onomatopoeia, simile, metaphor, imagery, hyperbole, rhythm)	7, 13, 24, 29
	6.8 Makes connections between characters or simple events in a literary work and people or events in his or her own life	All

Standards for Language Arts Grades 3–5 *(cont.)*

Standards	Benchmarks	Lesson
Uses reading skills and strategies to understand and interpret a variety of informational texts	7.5 Summarizes and paraphrases information in texts (e.g., includes the main idea and significant supporting details of a reading selection)	10
	7.7 Understands structural patterns or organization in informational texts (e.g., chronological, logical, or sequential order; compare and contrast; cause and effect, proposition and support)	26
Uses grammatical and mechanical conventions in written compositions	3.2 Uses pronouns in written compositions (e.g., substitutes pronouns for nouns, uses pronoun agreement)	3
	3.3 Uses nouns in written compositions (e.g., uses plural and singular naming words, forms regular and irregular plurals of nouns, uses common and proper nouns, uses nouns as subjects)	5, 16, 25
	3.4 Uses verbs in written compositions (e.g., uses a wide variety of action verbs, past and present verb tenses, simple tenses, forms of regular verbs, verbs that agree with subject)	4, 9, 16, 23, 25
	3.5 Uses adjectives in written compositions (e.g., indefinite, numerical, predicate adjectives)	5, 18, 27
	3.7 Uses coordinating conjunctions in written compositions (e.g., links ideas using connecting words)	21
	3.8 Uses negatives in written compositions (e.g., avoids double negatives)	28
	3.9 Uses conventions of spelling in written compositions (e.g., spells high frequency, commonly misspelled words from appropriate grade-level list; uses a dictionary and other resources to spell words; uses initial consonant substitution to spell related words; uses vowel combinations for correct spelling; uses contractions, compounds, roots, suffixes, prefixes, and syllable constructions to spell words)	11, 15
	3.10 Uses conventions of capitalization in written compositions (e.g., titles of people; proper nouns; first word of direct quotations; heading, salutation, and closing of a letter)	19
	3.11 Uses conventions of punctuation in written compositions (e.g., uses periods after imperative sentences and in initials, abbreviations, and titles before names; uses commas in dates and addresses and after greetings and closings in a letter; uses apostrophes in contractions and possessive nouns; uses quotation marks around titles and with direct quotations; uses a colon between hour and minutes)	1, 8, 17

Activity Skill—Correlation Chart

McREL Content Knowledge Standards for Language Arts Grades 3–5

Activity Page Title	Standards-Based Skill Focus	Page
Greetings (and Closings)	Punctuation—Greetings and Closings (3.11)	20
Character Comparison	Characterization (6.5)	24
That Pronoun Refers To…	Pronoun Referents (3.2)	28
Present or Past Participle	Recognizing Tense (3.4)	32
Noun or Adjective?	Nouns and Adjectives (3.3, 3.5)	36
Got the Rhythm?	Syllabication (5.4)	40
It's Like a Simile	Using Similes (6.7)	44
He Said, She Said	Quotation Marks—Dialogue (3.11)	48
I Do	Verb Agreement—Forms of Do (3.4)	52
Let's Summarize	Summarizing (7.5)	56
Compounding	Compound Words (3.9)	60
Just the Opposite	Antonyms (5.7)	64
Heart-y Expressions	Understanding Idioms (6.7, 8.6)	68
We're "Stuffed"	Practicing Fluency—Choral Reading (8.9)	72
Seeing Double	Double Consonant Patterns (3.9)	76
Naming and Doing	Parts of Speech—Noun/Verb (3.3, 3.4)	80
Straight from the Dog	Final Punctuation (3.11)	84
Describing Ghosts	Descriptive Adjectives (3.5)	88
Calendar Quest	Capitalization of Proper Nouns (3.10)	92
Read and Refrain	Practicing Fluency—Read and Refrain (8.9)	96
Coordinate Those Conjunctions	Coordinating Conjunctions (3.7)	100
There, Their, and They're	Homophones—There, Their, They're (5.7)	104
Changing Tense	Changing Tense (3.4)	108
Making Metaphors	Understanding Metaphors (6.7)	112
Is or Are?	Subject/Verb Agreement—Is/Are (3.3, 3.4)	116
Order, Please	Sequence (7.7)	120
More or Less Indefinite	Indefinite Adjectives (3.5)	124
No, Nothing, Never	Double Negatives (3.8)	128
Figuratively Speaking	Figurative Language (6.7)	132
What Do You Think?	Applying Comprehension Strategies (5.8, 5.10)	136

A Chorus of Voices

Although Mr. Witherspoon, Madison, and the rest of the students in Mrs. McBride's class are the acknowledged writers of "Dear Mr. Witherspoon," the real author is poet Brod Bagert. It is his voice heard in all the letters and poems.

Encouraged by his teacher, Brod Bagert wrote his first poem in the third grade and has been writing ever since. In high school, his relationship with poetry deepened as he struggled through the love-hate experience of reading the classics in the original Greek and Latin. As a university student, he was intrigued when another student from a neighboring college requested permission to publish two of his poems in her school's poetry review, an experience that led him to discover the power of poetry in the dating ritual.

The world then began to nibble away at Brod's love for poetry. He graduated from law school, married his high-school sweetheart, got elected to public office, and wrote fewer and fewer poems. Then, as a young father, he began to write poems for his own children to recite in their school programs. He was hooked. Deriving less and less satisfaction from a law practice and public career, poetry soon became his full-time occupation.

Brod is now the award-winning author of 17 books of poetry: 10 for children, two for young adults, and five for adults. He is also the author of an Edgar Allan Poe anthology and coauthor of the U.S. Department of Education's *Helping Your Child Learn to Read* (1993). He has appeared at hundreds of conferences, thousands of schools, and has performed his poetry in all 50 states and on five of the world's seven continents.

The heart of Brod's poetry is voice—not just his own voice, but a whole chorus of voices. In a poem for kindergartners, you will hear the voice of a kindergartner; in a poem for classroom teachers, you will hear the voice of a classroom teacher.

Brod's active performance schedule keeps him on the road about half the year. The other half he spends at home in New Orleans. He reads books, rides his bicycle, gardens with his wife, Debby, and dotes on their three rambunctious grandsons.

These poems are dedicated to Susie McBride.

—Brod Bagert

"Dear Mr. Witherspoon"

The letters and poems on which the lessons are based collectively comprise a book of their own—"Dear Mr. Witherspoon." The collection begins with a letter from Madison McDonald, a student in Mrs. McBride's class, who is having trouble finding a poem to recite that expresses how she feels. Mr. Witherspoon was a speaker (and promoter of poetry in the classroom) whom Mrs. McBride met in a summer class for teachers. Madison writes a letter to Mr. Witherspoon asking that he write a poem tailored for her. He does so, but also asks Madison not to tell the class because he doesn't have time to write a poem for everyone. Madison intends to comply, but lets it slip out to a friend, and Madison writes Mr. Witherspoon again, this time including personal notes and requests from every student in her class. After a bit of balking, Mr. Witherspoon concedes and writes a poem for every student in the class based on his or her individual letter of request. At the end, Mr. Witherspoon receives one more letter. This one is from another student who heard what he had done for Mrs. McBride's students and requests that he write poems for his class, too. Mr. Witherspoon declines with a bit of tongue-in-cheek humor.

Each poem is introduced with a letter from one of the students, which sets the stage for the poem. The letter reveals the student's musings—thoughts, feelings, or questions about life, the world, or just being a child. It tells the reader what inspired the poem, which encourages attentive listening, enhances comprehension, and undoubtedly creates a spontaneous audience response. It should also be noted that each poem is capable of functioning as a stand-alone piece. This unique style lends itself especially well to reading aloud and involving students in fluency exercises. The format provides built-in flexibility for the teacher and students. For example, if the poem is chosen for choral reading or for practice and performance, the letter still functions as dramatic direction.

As the letters and poems are read, it is easy to forget that Mr. Witherspoon, Madison, and the rest of the students are all the voice of poet Brod Bagert.

Madison's Request

This letter introduces a collection of poems by Mr. Witherspoon for the students in Mrs. McBride's class. Here, Madison McDonald writes Mr. Witherspoon asking him to write a poem for her.

Making Connections

- Prepare students to draw parallels from their own lives with what they will read. Ask students to take a moment to think about this question: When was a time that you felt frustrated because you couldn't find the right words to say how you felt? Ask students to share their experiences.

- Tell students that they are going to listen as you read a letter written by a student to a well-known poet. Ask students to connect their own experiences to Madison's as you read the letter.

Comprehension Strategy: Problem and Solution

- Distribute copies of the letter or display it for the class.

- Explain that one strategy for checking understanding is to try to identify the problem and the solution. Pair students and give them two minutes to identify the problem and solution in Madison's letter.

- Call on several pairs to share their answers. Encourage other students to respond to what is shared. If necessary, point out the problem: Madison cannot find an existing poem that says how she feels. Her solution is to ask a poet to write one just for her.

Standards-Based Skill Focus: Using Commas in Greetings and Closings of Letters

- Have students find the greeting and closing in the letter (Dear Mr. Witherspoon, and Sincerely,) and circle the commas.

- Have students complete the skill activity on individual copies of page 20.

Vocabulary Word Study

- Have students find and highlight the following words in the letter: *that's, can't you've, you're, it's, don't,* and *I'm*. Review that contractions are formed by combining two words into one and replacing one or more letters with an apostrophe.

- Challenge students to offer more examples of contractions. Then have students complete the word study activity on individual copies of page 21.

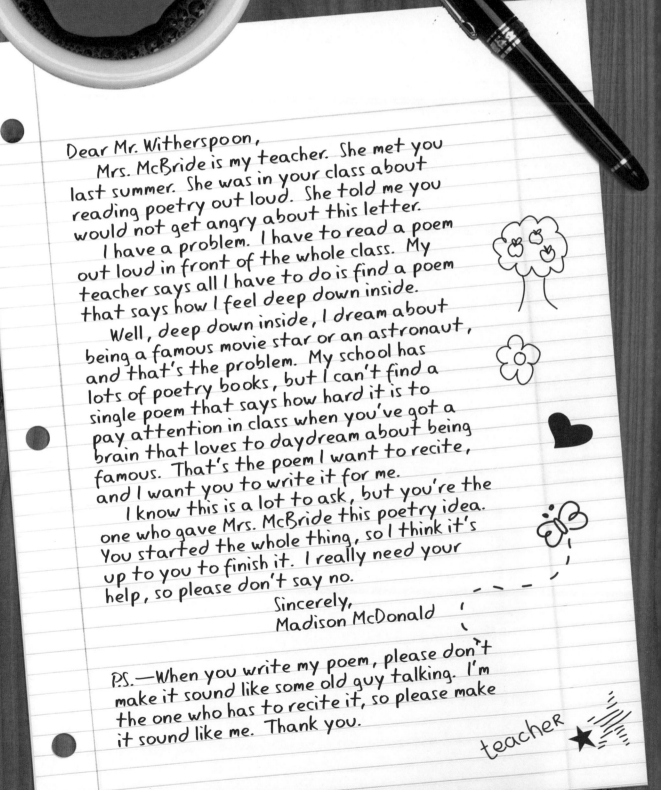

Dear Mr. Witherspoon,

Mrs. McBride is my teacher. She met you last summer. She was in your class about reading poetry out loud. She told me you would not get angry about this letter.

I have a problem. I have to read a poem out loud in front of the whole class. My teacher says all I have to do is find a poem that says how I feel deep down inside.

Well, deep down inside, I dream about being a famous movie star or an astronaut, and that's the problem. My school has lots of poetry books, but I can't find a single poem that says how hard it is to pay attention in class when you've got a brain that loves to daydream about being famous. That's the poem I want to recite, and I want you to write it for me.

I know this is a lot to ask, but you're the one who gave Mrs. McBride this poetry idea. You started the whole thing, so I think it's up to you to finish it. I really need your help, so please don't say no.

Sincerely,
Madison McDonald

P.S.—When you write my poem, please don't make it sound like some old guy talking. I'm the one who has to recite it, so please make it sound like me. Thank you.

teacher

Name:_____

Greetings (and Closings)

I. **Directions:** Read the letter Madison wrote to Mr. Witherspoon. Then complete each statement below.

    1. In a greeting and closing, the first word begins with a _____ letter.

    2. The punctuation mark at the end of a greeting and closing is a _____.

• •

II. **Directions:** Add the missing punctuation marks in the two letters that follow.

1. Dear Mrs. McBride

I wrote to Mr. Witherspoon to ask him to write a poem for me that expresses my feelings. I wanted just the right poem to read aloud in class.

           Your student

           Madison McDonald

2. Dear students

Last summer I took a class from a poet named Mr. Witherspoon. He suggested that we read poetry aloud in class. So, each of you needs to choose a poem to recite that expresses how you feel about something.

           Yours truly

           Mrs. McBride

Name: _____

Madison's Request

I. Directions: In her letter to Mr. Witherspoon, Madison used seven different contractions. Find and write them on the lines below.

_____   _____   _____

_____   _____

_____   _____

· ·

II. Directions: Each sentence below is missing one of the contractions you wrote above. Write the contraction that makes the most sense in the sentence.

My name is Madison and _____ having trouble finding a poem

that is just the right one for me to recite in class. Mr. Witherspoon, I think that

_____ a great poet! Since I _____ seem to find

a poem that suits me, I am asking you to write one for me. The poem should be

about having trouble sitting still in class, but _____ up to you what

the exact words should be. Just one more request—please _____ make

my poem sound like some old guy talking, okay?

Extension

Madison wants a poem about how she has trouble paying attention in class. If you were given Mrs. McBride's assignment, what would you want your poem to be about? Write two or three ideas that describe what your poem would be about.

Stuck

This letter and poem is the first in the collection of poems by Mr. Witherspoon for the students in Mrs. McBride's class. Here, Mr. Witherspoon answers Madison's request and includes a poem for her.

Making Connections

- Prepare students to draw parallels from their own lives with what they will read. Ask students to take a moment to think about someone they know whom they would describe as shy. Then students should select a person they would describe as the opposite (bold and outgoing). Then, without naming any particular person, ask volunteers to offer reasons why they would characterize a person as shy or bold.

- Tell students they will listen as you read a letter and poem by Mr. Witherspoon. Ask them to think of characteristics that Madison displayed in her request letter and what Mr. Witherspoon seems to be like based on his response.

Comprehension Strategy: Clarify

- Distribute copies of the letter and poem or display them for the class.

- Help students clarify their understanding of the poem by discussing these questions: What does Mr. Witherspoon not usually do? Why did Mr. Witherspoon decide to make an exception and do it for one student? What did Mr. Witherspoon ask Madison not to tell her classmates? Why? Does Mr. Witherspoon's poem for Madison fulfill her request? Why or why not?

Standards-Based Skill Focus: Characterization

- Write the words *shy* and *bold* on the board. Ask students which characteristic best describes Madison. Then ask students to suggest other character traits that would describe a person. Record these on the board. If necessary, provide a few to get them started, such as *daring*, *generous*, *polite*, *grouchy*, *bossy*, and *serious*.

- Have students use the list to complete the skill activity on individual copies of page 24.

Vocabulary Word Study

- Have students find and highlight the following words in the letter and poem: *write*, *know*, *wrote*, *whole*, *could*, *would*, *watch*, and *half*. Point out that all of these words have silent letters. Ask students to verbally identify the silent letter(s) in each word.

- Challenge students to name other words they know that have silent letters. Ask volunteers to spell the words and identify the silent letter(s).

- Have students complete the word study activity on individual copies of page 25.

Dear Miss McDonald,

Thank you for your very interesting letter. I don't usually write poems on request, but I like what you said about not being able to sit still. I know how that feels, and you did say please, so here's your poem.

You can tell your teacher I wrote this poem especially for you, but please do not tell your classmates. I'm a very busy person and I do not have time to write poems for a whole classroom full of children.

Sincerely,
Mr. Witherspoon

Stuck

If I could be a famous star, a famous movie queen,
the world would watch me acting on the giant silver screen!
I'd have half a dozen houses. I'd have twenty-seven cars.
I'd have twice as many loyal fans as all the other stars.

If I could be an astronaut, a rocket-riding ace,
I'd put a shiny spacesuit on and soar out into space.
I'd flutter like a feather. I'd float like a balloon.
I'd fly a girl-manned missile, and I'd land it on the moon.

Oh, all the things I'd love to do, it's such a lovely dream;
but I'm stuck here in this classroom, and it makes me want to scream.

Name:_____

Character Comparison

Directions: This diagram can be used to compare characters. Use what you know about Madison and Mr. Witherspoon to complete it. Follow these steps:

1. In the part of the circle labeled *Madison*, write two traits that she has.

2. In the part of the circle labeled *Mr. Witherspoon*, write two traits that he has.

3. In the overlapping part of the circles, write one trait that they both have.

4. In the area outside of the circles, write at least one trait that neither has.

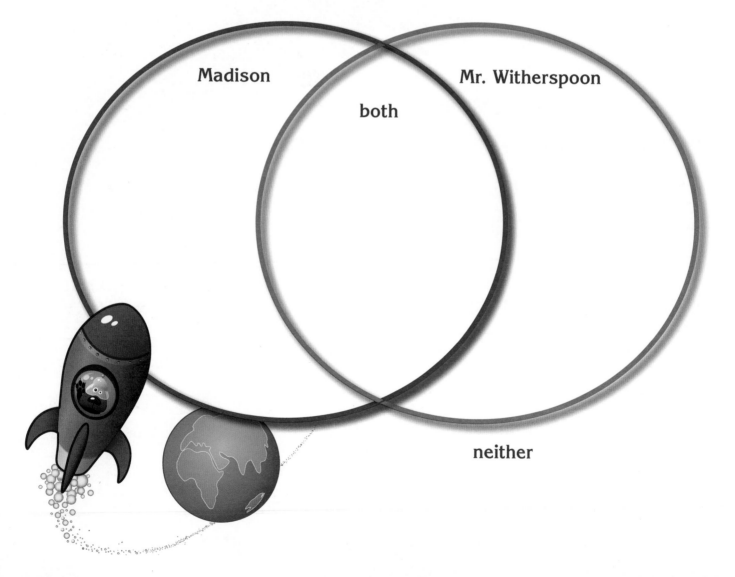

Madison   Mr. Witherspoon

both

neither

Name: _____

Stuck

I. Directions: Read these words. Circle any word that has at least one silent letter.

know	castle	twenty	would	knife	wrestle
talk	last	listen	watch	Lincoln	half
knee	answer	wrote	kneel	how	kitten
sink	whole	could	often	knot	calf

• •

II. Directions: Write each word you circled above in the column that tells which letter—*l, t, k,* or *w*—is silent in the word.

Silent l	Silent t	Silent k	Silent w
_____	_____	_____	_____
_____	_____	_____	_____
_____	_____	_____	_____
_____	_____	_____	_____
_____	_____	_____	_____
_____	_____	_____	_____

Extension

The letters *l, t, k,* and *w* are not the only letters that can be silent. There are several others. Copy these words in big print on a sheet of paper: *lamb, raspberry, sign, ghost, island,* and *Wednesday.* Then find and highlight with a marker or crayon the silent letters in them.

Madison's Reply

In the previous lesson, Mr. Witherspoon replied to Madison and wrote a poem for her. He thinks that is the end of it, but Madison writes to him again. Here is Madison's reply to Mr. Witherspoon.

Making Connections

- Prepare students to draw parallels from their own lives with what they will read. Ask students to think about a time when they were asked to keep a secret. Is it okay to have secrets? Should a secret be kept no matter what? Why or why not? What reason might someone have for sharing a secret? Give students time to reflect. Then call on various students to answer.

- Tell students they will listen as you read the follow-up letter from Madison to Mr. Witherspoon.

Comprehension Strategy: The 5 Ws

- Distribute copies of the letter or display it for the class.

- Write five capital Ws in a column on the board. Explain that a good way to check understanding of what is read is to ask the 5 Ws. As you identify them as *what, who/ whom, where, when,* and *why,* complete each word on the board. Then challenge students to answer these 5 W questions:

  1. WHAT was the secret?

  2. WHOM did Madison tell?

  3. WHERE were they when she told?

  4. WHEN did the secret slip out?

  5. WHY is Madison asking for 25 more poems?

Standards-Based Skill Focus: Pronoun Referents

- Remind students that words such as *she, he, it, I, you, me, we, us, them,* and *they* are called *pronouns* and take the place of names of people, places, or things.

- Have students identify as many pronouns as they can in the poem. Discuss which noun/name each pronoun refers to.

- Distribute copies of page 28 for students to complete individually or with a partner. Later, ask a few volunteers to share their responses.

Vocabulary Word Study

- Have students find and highlight the following words in the letter: *perfect, yesterday, totally, unfair, special,* and *written.* Clarify meanings as needed.

- Distribute copies of page 29 and have students use the clues to complete the puzzle. Depending on your students' needs, you can decide whether to allow them to refer to the letter for help as they work the puzzle.

Dear Mr. Witherspoon,

Thank you so much for the poem. It was almost perfect, but now we have another problem. I know I wasn't supposed to tell the other kids, but Morgan Kernion is my best friend and I just had to tell her. Then yesterday morning on the school bus she sort of let it slip out, and now everybody knows, and everybody thinks it would be totally unfair if I were the only one who got a special poem.

We have 26 students in our class, and we'll need one poem for each of us. You've already written one for me, so you only have to write 25 more. We know this is a lot of work, but writing poems is your job, so please help us.

Your friend,
Madison McDonald

P.S.—Along with this letter, we're sending you a bunch of notes from our whole class telling you how each of us feels and what we want our poems to be about.

Thank you!
★ FUN WOW 👓

Name: _____

That Pronoun Refers To...

Directions: Below is a copy of the main part of Madison's second letter to Mr. Witherspoon. As you read it, pay special attention to the words in bold print. When you finish reading, go back to the numbered words, which are pronouns. Then, on the lines below, write what each pronoun stands for.

Dear Mr. Witherspoon,

Thank you so much for the poem. **It**① was almost perfect, but now we have another problem. **I**② know I wasn't supposed to tell the other kids, but Morgan Kernion is my best friend and I just had to tell **her**③. Then yesterday morning on the school bus **she**④ sort of let **it**⑤ slip out, and now everybody knows, and everybody thinks it would be totally unfair if I were the only **one**⑥ who got a special poem.

We have 26 students in our class, and we'll need one poem for each of **us**⑦. You've already written one for me, so **you**⑧ only have to write 25 more. We know this is a lot of work, but writing poems is your job, so please help us.

Your friend,

Madison McDonald

1. What is **it**? _____

2. Who is **I**? _____

3. Who is **her**? _____

4. Who is **she**? _____

5. What is **it**? _____

6. What is **one?** _____

7. Who is **us**? _____

8. Who is **you**? _____

Name:_____

Madison's Reply

Directions: Solve the crossword puzzle below with words from Madison's letter of reply to Mr. Witherspoon.

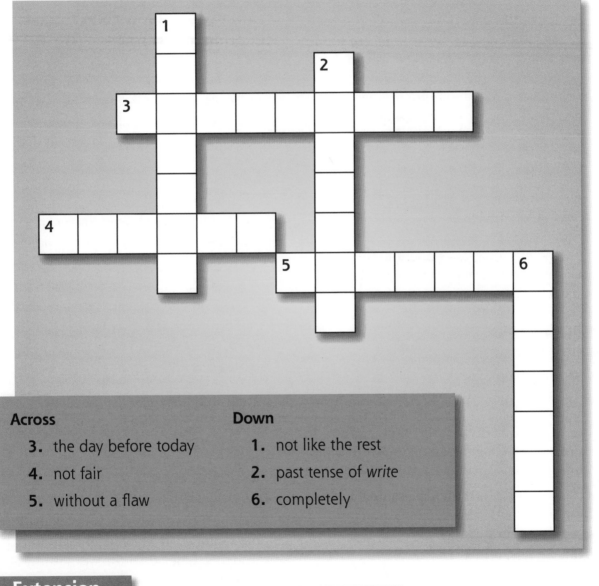

Across

3. the day before today

4. not fair

5. without a flaw

Down

1. not like the rest

2. past tense of *write*

6. completely

Extension

Use each of the six words in sentences of your own.

Mr. Witherspoon's Response

Mr. Witherspoon responds to Madison's second letter with a letter of his own. Although he expresses that he did not want to write 25 more poems, he explains why he is doing it.

Making Connections

- Prepare students to draw parallels from their own lives with what they will read. Ask students to think about a time when they dreaded doing something—especially because it either seemed too hard or would take too long. Give students time to reflect and then call on various volunteers to share their experiences.

- Tell students they will listen as you read the letter Mr. Witherspoon sent in response to Madison's request that he write poems for every student in the class. Ask students to make predictions about what Mr. Witherspoon might have said.

Comprehension Strategy: Making Inferences

- Distribute copies of the letter or display it for the class. Explain that good readers sometimes have to "read between the lines"—figure out what the writer was thinking or feeling based on the words and phrases used.

- Discuss what Mr. Witherspoon might have been thinking or feeling when he used these phrases: *all because of you*; *you and your little friends*; *over and over and over*; and *have written for a whole week*. Point out that different readers may have different interpretations of what they read. Encourage students to share their thoughts and reasons for them.

Standards-Based Skill Focus: Recognizing Tense

- Teach or reinforce the difference between present participle and past participle. Remind students that present participle verbs show action that is happening now. Past participle verbs show action that has already happened.

- On the board, draw two columns and label them *Present Participle* and *Past Participle*. Write the words *starting* and *started* in the correct columns and explain why you are doing so.

- Have students complete the skill focus activity on individual copies of page 32. Save the chart for the word study activity on page 33.

Vocabulary Word Study

- Help students use what they have learned about tense to expand their word knowledge.

- Work as a group to find and highlight the following words in the letter: *slept*, *requesting*, *hearing*, *saying*, *trying*, and *written*. As you find each word, read the sentence in which it appears and ask students to decide if the word is present participle or past participle. Add the words to the columns on the board.

- Before having students complete the word study activity on individual copies of page 33, erase the words from the board.

Dear Miss McDonald,

I haven't slept for a week and it's all because of you—you and your little friends and those brain-tickling letters. I read your letter first and thought: Twenty-five new poems? No way! Then I read the notes from your classmates. The last one I read was the one from Vivian Campanelli requesting a lollipop poem. I thought to myself: Isn't that cute, but still—NO WAY! I put the letters away and tried to go to sleep, but every time I closed my eyes I kept hearing Vivian Campanelli's voice in my head saying the word *lollipop* over and over and over. It wouldn't stop until I got out of bed and wrote a lollipop poem.

Now I'll get some sleep, I thought. But as soon as I closed my eyes, I heard a new voice. This time it was Bobby Gill and the word was *recess*, so I started writing a recess poem. And by the time it was finished, my head was full of voices, each one trying to turn itself into a poem. I wrote all night long, poem after poem. I wrote all the next day and that night too and the next day. I have written for a whole week, and finally I'm finished.

So here they are—25 new poems, one for each of your classmates. I'm glad I wrote them, but this is the end of it. So please do not write to me again.

Sincerely,

Mr. Witherspoon

Name:_____

Present or Past Participle

Directions: Read each sentence and the pair of verbs. Choose the correct verb and write it on the line.

1. He had _____ on the science project all night.
   (working, worked)

2. Mom is out _____ something for dinner.
   (getting, got)

3. I am _____ a thank-you note to my aunt.
   (writing, written)

4. Grandma had _____ all my old baby pictures.
   (keeping, kept)

5. She is _____ the door.
   (closing, closed)

6. Most cats are _____ during the day.
   (sleeping, slept)

7. I wasn't done, so I had _____ for more time.
   (asking, asked)

8. She had _____ to school that morning.
   (walking, walked)

Name:_____

Mr. Witherspoon's Response

Directions: Every word on the chart below is a past participle verb Mr. Witherspoon used in his letter of response to Madison McDonald. Write the present participle of each word. The first one is done for you to get you started—*slept* is the past tense of *sleep*.

	Past Participle	Present Participle
1.	slept	sleeping
2.	read	
3.	thought	
4.	tried	
5.	kept	
6.	got	
7.	finished	
8.	closed	

Extension

Are you more like Madison or Mr. Witherspoon? Why?

Pop!

Mr. Witherspoon has received letters from every student requesting a poem. Vivian's letter asking for a lollipop poem is what inspired Mr. Witherspoon to write all the poems. Here is Vivian's letter and the poem Mr. Witherspoon wrote for her.

Making Connections

- Prepare students to draw parallels from their own lives with what they will read. Ask students to think of a time when they described something using exaggeration, such as swimming a mile or eating a ton of pizza. Give students time to reflect and then share their descriptions in pairs.

- Tell students that they are going to listen as you read a letter from one of Madison's classmates and the poem Mr. Witherspoon wrote for her. Ask students to listen for Mr. Witherspoon's uses of exaggerations.

Comprehension Strategy: Imagery

- Distribute copies of the letter and poem or display them for the class.

- Explain that writers use words and phrases to create images in readers' minds. Ask students to identify examples of this in the poem.

- Write the following frame on the board: I like _____ , as big as _____. Challenge students to come up with their own words to fill in the blanks. Call on several students to share their answers.

Standards-Based Skill Focus: Nouns and Adjectives

- Have students underline all 11 uses of the word *lollipop* in the poem. Then point out that *lollipop* is used two different ways—as a noun, or naming word, and as an adjective, or describing word.

- As a group, review every use of the word and determine if it is used as a noun or an adjective.

- Have students complete the skill activity on individual copies of page 36.

Vocabulary Word Study

- Explain that adjectives often describe something to do with the senses. They tell how something looks, feels, tastes, smells, or sounds. Find examples in the poem (*big, red, blue, sweet,* and *stinky*). Have students broaden their understanding of the functions of words by generating and classifying descriptive words.

- Distribute copies of page 37. Explain that words from the poem have been classified under headings that tell about the senses. Challenge students to add at least three words to each of the five categories.

Dear Mr. Witherspoon,

I like lollipops. I like the way they taste. I like the bright colors they come in. I even like the way the word feels when I say it. Lollipop! Lollipop! Please write a lollipop poem for me.

Your friend,
Vivian Campanelli

Pop!

I want lollipops, if you please.
I want lollipops, BIG AS TREES!
I want lollipops—red and blue.
One for me and one for you!

Lollipop garden! Lollipop house!
Lollipop cat and a lollipop mouse!
Lollipop girls are oh so sweet.
Lollipop boys have stinky feet!

I want lollipops! Yes-sir-ee!
One for you and two for me.
I eat! I eat! I cannot stop!
I eat until I lolli-POP!

Name: _____

Noun or Adjective?

Directions: Read each sentence. Decide if the word in bold print is used as a noun (naming word) or an adjective (describing word). Write *noun* or *adjective* on the line.

Examples: I want **lollipops**, if you please. <u>noun (names something)</u>
 Lollipop girls are oh so sweet. <u>adjective (describes something)</u>

1. The **apple** is my favorite fruit. _____

2. My favorite dessert is **apple** pie. _____

3. I like to make **paper** airplanes. _____

4. I am really good at folding **paper**. _____

5. Last night I ate until my **stomach** was full. _____

6. This morning I woke up with **stomach** pains. _____

7. Mom said I ate too many **potato** chips. _____

8. A **potato** is a vegetable that grows underground. _____

9. Someday I hope to get a **puppy**. _____

10. How could anyone resist those cute **puppy** eyes? _____

Name:_____

Pop!

Directions: Many words tell how something looks, feels, tastes, smells, or sounds. These are called *sensory words* because they tell about the senses. Mr. Witherspoon used six sensory words in Vivian's poem. They appear in the categories below. Your job is to think of and write at least three more sensory words in each category to describe a lollipop.

LOOKS	big, red, blue
FEELS	
TASTES	sweet
SMELLS	stinky
SOUNDS	

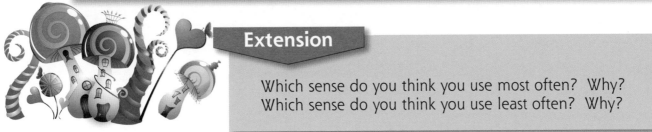

Extension

Which sense do you think you use most often? Why?
Which sense do you think you use least often? Why?

The Recess Song

This is the third in a collection of poems by Mr. Witherspoon for the students in Mrs. McBride's class. Here, Bobby has requested a poem about his favorite part of the day. Mr. Witherspoon fulfills his request with "The Recess Song."

Making Connections

- Prepare students to draw parallels from their own lives with what they will read. On the board, write *breakfast*, *school*, *recess*, *lunch*, *playing*, *dinner*, and *family time*. Ask students to vote for their favorite activity of the day. Tally the results. Then ask students to comment on either their favorite part of the day or the results.

- Tell students that they will listen to a letter from Bobby and the poem Mr. Witherspoon wrote for him, "The Recess Song."

Comprehension Strategy: Elements of Genre—Poetry

- Distribute copies of the letter and poem or display them for the class.

- Ask students to suggest ways the letter and the poem are alike and different. Explain that, although they are both about recess, a major difference is how they are presented. The letter and poem each has certain features. Challenge students to identify some of these features.

- Focus on the element of rhythm in poetry. Have students read the poem aloud several times. Ask students to clap out the rhythm as they read.

Standards-Based Skill Focus: Syllabication

- Help students connect what they have learned about rhythm to syllabication. Explain that the beats of a word correspond to the number of syllables in it.

- Write the following words on the board: *wait*, *recess*, and *Witherspoon*. Have students clap the beats of each word. After saying that one clap equals one syllable, have students tell how many syllables are in each word.

- Have students complete the skill activity on individual copies of page 40.

Vocabulary Word Study

- Follow up on your study of rhythm and syllables by having students make connections between words. First, as a group, have students brainstorm a list of things they like. Record these on the board.

- After there are at least 15 things listed, have students clap out each word and identify the number of syllables.

- Leave this list on the board and distribute copies of page 41. Review the two-part directions, and then let students have fun completing the activity.

Dear Mr. Witherspoon,

Recess is what I like the most. It's my favorite part of the day. I get to run around outside with my all friends and play. The only thing I don't like about recess is that it has to end.

Your friend,
Bobby Gill

The Recess Song

Recess! Recess! You're so great!
Recess, I can hardly wait!

Recess! Recess! Finally here!
Now I shout a recess cheer!

Recess…recess…gone again…
Why does recess have to end?

Time to sing my recess song—
I WANT RECESS ALL DAY LONG!

Name:_____

Got the Rhythm?

I. Directions: Below is a copy of Bobby's letter to Mr. Witherspoon. Above each word, write the number of syllables in the word. If necessary, clap out the rhythm to determine the number of syllables. The greeting is done to get you started.

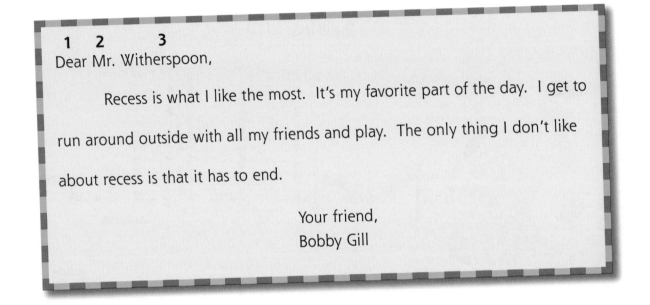

1 2   3
Dear Mr. Witherspoon,

   Recess is what I like the most. It's my favorite part of the day. I get to

run around outside with all my friends and play. The only thing I don't like

about recess is that it has to end.

                              Your friend,
                              Bobby Gill

- -

II. Directions: Answer the questions. Use evidence from the letter to support your answers.

1. Do all one-syllable words have four letters or less? _____

Prove it. _____

_____

2. Do all two-syllable words have more than four letters? _____

Prove it. _____

_____

Name: _____

The Recess Song

I. **Directions:** On the lines below, write the names of six things you like. Wait! There's a catch. Each word can have only two syllables—no more, no less—such as *recess*, *football*, *sleeping*, and *Sunday*.

_____ _____ _____

_____ _____ _____

• •

II. **Directions:** Use Bobby's poem as a frame to make your own poem. Fill in the blanks with one of the things you like. Remember—two-syllable words only!

The _____ Song

_____! _____! You're so great!

_____, I can hardly wait.

_____! _____! Finally here!

Now I shout a _____ cheer.

_____..._____...gone again...

Why does _____ have to end?

Time to sing my _____ song—

I WANT _____ ALL DAY LONG!

Extension

Practice reading your poem aloud until you can read it with perfect rhythm.
Then read it like a performance for someone in your family.

The One

The next letter to Mr. Witherspoon is from Han Jung. He wants a poem that expresses how empowered he feels while playing video games because it is something he is very good at. Mr. Witherspoon obliges with the poem "The One."

Making Connections

- Prepare students to draw parallels from their own lives with what they will read. Ask students to think of something that they are especially good at and how it makes them feel when they do it. Offer an example such as "I'm really good at singing. When I sing, I feel like a star." Give students time to reflect and then call on various students to share their thoughts and ideas.

- Tell students they will listen as you read a letter from Han and the poem Mr. Witherspoon wrote for him, "The One."

Comprehension Strategy: Figurative Language

- Distribute copies of the letter and poem or display them for the class.

- Explain that sometimes writers use phrases that do not mean what the words actually say. The reader must figure out the true meaning.

- Point out the following phrases from the poem: *just skin and bone, live inside the game*, and *get to be the one*. Ask students to speculate what each of these phrases actually means.

- Conclude by reminding students that good readers make sure that they understand not just the words they read, but also the author's intended meaning.

Standards-Based Skill Focus: Using Similes

- Teach or remind students that similes are comparisons using *like* or *as*. Give an example or two, such as *floating like a cloud* and *as soft as silk*. Challenge students to come up with more examples.

- Draw students' attention to the second stanza of the poem and ask a volunteer to read it aloud. Explain that Mr. Witherspoon used similes to tell how Han feels when he plays video games.

- Have students complete the skill activity on individual copies of page 44 for extra practice at recognizing and using similes.

Vocabulary Word Study

- Have students find and highlight the following words in the poem: *cheetah, capture, rescue*, and *conquer*. Clarify meanings by asking these questions: 1) Is a *cheetah* a type of cat or a type of cracker? 2) Which means the same as *capture*— release or catch? 3) Would someone lost want to be *rescued* or not? Why? 4) Would you want to *conquer* an enemy or a friend? Why?

- Have students complete the word study activity on individual copies of page 45.

Dear Mr. Witherspoon,

I do my homework, I get good grades, and I like sports. But I also love to play video games, and I wish I could explain it to my mother. I wish I could make her understand how cool it feels to be in the game and to be really good at it, like you're a total hero.

Your friend,
Han Jung

THE ONE

I'm really just a little kid,
just skin and bone like you,
but when I play computer games
there's nothing I can't do.

As fast as a flash,
as quick as a spark—
I run like a cheetah!
I swim like a shark!

I capture the bad guys
and rescue the girl!
I conquer the monsters
and save the whole world!

And that is why I play these games
hour after hour,
'cause when I live inside the game
my heart is pumping power.

So I like books and I like school,
and sports are lots of fun,
but when I play computer games
I get to be…THE ONE!

Name:_____

It's Like a Simile

I. Directions: In the poem "The One," Han is just a regular kid in real life, but when he enters the world of computer games, he feels special, powerful, and important. Read the lines from the poem below. Then go back and underline all the similes.

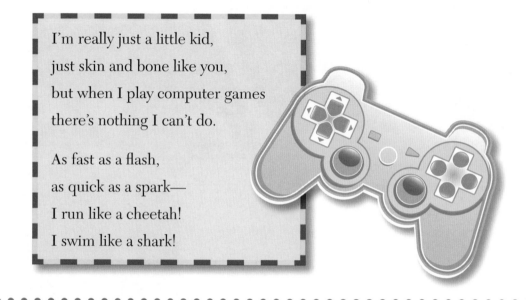

I'm really just a little kid,

just skin and bone like you,

but when I play computer games

there's nothing I can't do.

As fast as a flash,

as quick as a spark—

I run like a cheetah!

I swim like a shark!

• •

II. Directions: Think of something you are good at. Use the frame from Han's poem below. Fill in your own words to make it a poem about you.

I'm really just a little kid, just skin and bone like you,

But when I _____,

there's nothing I can't do.

As _____ as a _____,

As _____ as a _____—

I _____ like a _____!

I _____ like a _____!

Name:_____

The One

Directions: Below are four words you read in Han's poem, "The One." Choose the correct word to fill in the blank of each sentence.

cheetah	capture	rescue	conquer

1. I like science fiction movies—especially ones in which monster aliens come from space in order to _____ Earth.

2. The monster aliens are always the bad guys, and I like to see how the Earth people manage to _____ the aliens.

3. As soon as all the people see the alien monster coming, they start running like a rabbit runs from a _____.

4. In these movies, the Earth people are in danger, and just before the monster aliens get them, the hero comes to the _____.

Extension

The title of Han's poem is "The One." Why do you think Mr. Witherspoon chose that title, and what does it mean?

The Cure

The next letter to Mr. Witherspoon is from Morgan Kernion. She asks for a poem about being a "wimp" when it comes to pain. Mr. Witherspoon's response? A poem called "The Cure."

Making Connections

- Prepare students to draw parallels from their own lives with what they will read. Have a few students offer ideas about what it means to be a wimp. Then ask students to think of something they are a wimp about. Get them started with an example such as "I like to watch the rides at amusement parks, but I'm a wimp when it comes to getting on a roller coaster." Give students time to reflect and then call on various volunteers to share their thoughts.

- Tell students that they will listen as you read a letter from Morgan and the poem Mr. Witherspoon wrote for her, "The Cure." Afterward, ask students if they think Morgan is a wimp or not, and why.

Comprehension Strategy: Cause and Effect

- Distribute copies of the letter and poem or display them for the class.

- Clarify the terms *cause* and *effect*. Explain that a cause is the reason for something and an effect is the result. Give this example from the poem: Cause—afraid to pull a splinter; Effect—foot swollen and walking with a limp.

- Ask students to reread the second stanza, which describes how the writer swallowed her tooth. What is the cause? (*She was scared and refused to let her dad pull out the loose tooth.*)

Standards-Based Skill Focus: Quotation Marks—Dialogue

- Write the word *dialogue* on the board. Explain that dialogue is simply a conversation between people. When dialogue is written, quotation marks are used to set apart words that are spoken by characters from words that tell the story.

- Have students find the quotation marks in the poem, identify who is speaking, and what is said.

- Distribute copies of page 48. Read the story aloud. Direct students to insert quotation marks around each part that represents dialogue.

Vocabulary Word Study

- Have students find and highlight the following words in the letter and poem: *splinter, wimp, swollen, limp, swallowed,* and *cure*. Clarify the meanings of the words as needed.

- Explain to students that they are going to play a game of "I'm thinking of…." Be sure that students have access to a copy of the poem (their own or the one on display).

- Distribute copies of page 49. Review the directions and have students complete the activity on their own.

Dear Mr. Witherspoon,
I'm not afraid to try new things, and I'm not afraid of the dark. But when it comes to pain, I'm a total wimp. I can't even pull a splinter.

Your friend,
Morgan Kernion

PRESCRIPTION BLANK

Rx

The Cure

I'm afraid to pull a splinter.
I'm such a total wimp—
that's why my foot's all swollen
and I'm walking with a limp.

"You should let me pull that tooth," Dad said.
"It's wiggling like jelly."
"NO!" I said and swallowed it,
and now it's in my belly.

I know what I'm supposed to do,
I'm absolutely sure,
but even though I know what's best,
I'm frightened of the cure.

SUBSTITUTION PERMISSIBLE   DO NOT SUBSTITUTE

DO NOT REFILL   SIGNATURE OF PRESCRIBER

REFILL   TIMES

Name:_____

He Said, She Said

Directions: Below is a story about what might have taken place between Morgan and her dad when he wanted to pull her loose tooth. Find the parts in the story that are someone's exact words—what would have been said out loud. Add quotation marks before and after each part that is someone's exact words.

Dad walked into the kitchen where Morgan was already sitting at the table. Good morning, Dad said.

Morgan grumbled and just stirred her cereal around. What's the matter? asked Dad. Why aren't you eating?

I can't. My tooth is so loose that I am afraid that I will swallow it, said Morgan. What would happen if I swallow it, Dad?

Dad thought for a moment. Probably nothing, he finally said. But, maybe you should let me pull it out.

No way! exclaimed Morgan.

Okay, said Dad. Just let me see how loose it is.

As Dad stepped toward Morgan to look, she shut her mouth and swallowed hard. Then she smiled. You can look now, Dad, she said.

Dad looked in Morgan's mouth but didn't see a loose tooth. Where is it? he asked.

Morgan smiled again. That's for me to know and you to find out, she said with a sly smile.

Name:_____

The Cure

Directions: The answer to each riddle below is in Morgan's poem, "The Cure." Read each riddle and find the answer in the poem. Write it on the line.

1. I am a word with two syllables that is the adjective form of *swell*.
   What am I? _____

2. We are a pair of rhyming words. One of us is a scaredy-cat. The other walks with a hobble.
   What are we? _____

3. I describe a thin sliver of wood, metal, glass, or other material broken off from a larger piece.
   What am I? _____

4. I am the treatment, what heals someone sick, or brings an end to a problem.
   What am I? _____

5. I am an action word that tells how something got from your mouth to your stomach. What am I? _____

6. I mean "moving around." What am I? _____

Extension

The last line of the poem "The Cure" says, "I'm frightened of the cure." Explain what you think that means.

A Natural Bodily Function

The next letter to Mr. Witherspoon is from Lenny MacIntyre. He wonders why his classmates all seem to laugh at disgusting stuff. Mr. Witherspoon understands and provides the poem "A Natural Bodily Function."

Making Connections

- Prepare students to draw parallels from their own lives with what they will read. Ask students to think of a time when they got the giggles because they were embarrassed. Give an example such as, "Once I was at a wedding and the bride tripped on her dress. I instantly got the giggles." Give students time to reflect and then share their thoughts in pairs.

- Tell students that they will listen as you read a letter from Lenny about laughing at an embarrassing thing and the poem Mr. Witherspoon wrote for him, "A Natural Bodily Function."

Comprehension Strategy: Shades of Meaning

- Distribute copies of the letter and poem or display them for the class.

- Point out that, like colors, words have different shades of meaning and writers use them to make their writing more precise. Say the words *gold*, *mustard*, *canary*, and *daffodil* and ask what these all describe (color—shades of yellow). Write *giggle* and *laugh* on the board. Ask students if these mean exactly the same thing, and if not, what the difference is.

- Repeat with these word pairs: *shout/say* and *disgusting/unpleasant*.

Standards-Based Skill Focus: Verb Agreement—Forms of "Do"

- Write the following pronouns and verbs on the board: *he do; she do; it do; I does; I doesn't; he don't; she don't; it don't; they does;* and *they doesn't*. Ask students if they have ever said or heard these used.

- Cross out *he do* and replace with *he does* while saying, "Never 'he do', always 'he does'." Have students repeat it after you in unison. Continue in the same manner crossing out and replacing the incorrect verb forms and having students repeat the correct uses.

- Distribute copies of page 52. Tell students to keep in mind what they learned about using *do*, *does*, *don't*, and *doesn't* as they complete the activity.

Vocabulary Word Study

- Help students understand how words are related. Review the concept of word families—groups of words that rhyme and have the same spelling patterns.

- Distribute copies of page 53, which uses words from the poem to challenge students to generate other words in the same family. Then have students complete the activity on their own.

Dear Mr. Witherspoon,
    I don't know why but I always laugh at disgusting stuff. And it's not just me, it's almost everybody. I just don't understand it.
                    Your friend,
                    Lenny MacIntyre

A Natural Bodily Function

Why do they always giggle?
It's every kid in class!
Why do they think it's funny
when I pass a little gas?

They don't giggle when I hiccup,
they don't giggle when I sneeze,
but if I sneak a little squeak they shout—
WHO CUT THE CHEESE?

It's a natural bodily function,
a healthy little toot,
so why do people giggle
when a person makes a poot?

Name:_____

I Do

Directions: Do you ever get confused about when to use *do* or *does*? How about when to use *don't* or *doesn't*? This chart will guide you. Use the chart to help you choose and write the correct verb in each sentence.

I, They	He, She, It
do	does
don't	doesn't

1. He _____ his homework right after school. (do/does)

2. They _____ have any pets. (don't/doesn't)

3. To help out, every evening I _____ the dishes. (do/does)

4. It _____ rain much in the desert. (don't/doesn't)

5. The man said that it _____ come with a case. (do/does)

6. I _____ like beets. (don't/doesn't)

7. On Saturday, I _____ my chores. (do/does)

8. She _____ have any aunts or uncles. (don't/doesn't)

9. They _____ still have tickets for the game. (do/does)

10. He _____ need a haircut yet. (don't/doesn't)

Name: _____

A Natural Bodily Function

Directions: Each word below is from the poem "A Natural Bodily Function." Your job is to write as many more words as you can in the same word family. The first one is started for you.

Word from the Poem	Other Words in the Same Word Family
1. class	grass, pass
2. giggle	
3. sneeze	
4. sneak	
5. think	
6. shout	
7. toot	

Extension

You can use word families to help you write your own poems. For example, how would you finish this one?

    Sometimes in class I break out in a giggle.

    If I have to sit too long, I start to squirm and _____.

Now use one or more of the word families you created on the chart to write a new poem of your own.

Watch Out!

The next letter to Mr. Witherspoon is from Laura Akerman. Laura wants a poem about her cool new shoes. Mr. Witherspoon's poem "Watch Out!" tells how she learned a lesson from a close encounter with a car.

Making Connections

- Prepare students to draw parallels from their own lives with what they will read. Ask students to think of a time when they learned a lesson by having a "close encounter" or a "close call"—an accident or situation that could have turned out much worse than it did. Give students time to reflect and then call on various students to share their thoughts.

- Tell students that they will listen as you read a letter from Laura and the poem Mr. Witherspoon wrote for her, "Watch Out!"

Comprehension Strategy: Sequence

- Distribute copies of the letter and poem or display them for the class.

- Direct students' attention to the last two couplets. Ask what lesson was learned and what advice is given at the end of the poem. (*Watch out for cars when crossing the street.*) Explain that to lead up to that advice, the poem explains step-by-step what happened.

- Ask students to use the words *First*, *Next*, *Then*, and *Last* to paraphrase the first four stanzas. Remind students that reviewing the sequence, or order of events, is a good way to make sure they understand the story and do not miss the important elements.

Standards-Based Skill Focus: Summarizing

- Write the following words on the board: *First*, *Next*, *Then*, and *Last*. Explain that these words signal the order (or sequence) of things, and using these words is a good way to summarize the main elements.

- Use the activity "Let's Summarize" on page 56 to give students the opportunity to practice summarizing. Have students work alone or in pairs to complete the activity.

Vocabulary Word Study

- Point out that prepositions are used to make phrases that tell how, where, when, or why. Ask students to help you make a short list of prepositions on the board.

- Make sure that students have access to the poem for reference. Then distribute copies of page 57. Explain to students that they will need to refer to the poem to find the answers on the activity sheet.

Dear Mr. Witherspoon,
    I got new shoes that look so cool on my feet I just want to look at them all the time.

                                Your friend,
                                Laura Akerman

WATCH OUT!

I got some new sneakers that look really cool,
so I laced them up tight, and I headed for school.

I stood on the curb at the edge of the street,
but I kept looking down at those shoes on my feet.

When I saw the light change, I was off with a bound.
But the next thing I knew, I had flipped upside down.

The screeching of tires! The crunching of steel!
A shiny chrome bumper! A black rubber wheel!

And then I woke up in a hospital bed
with a cast on my leg and a bump on my head.

Now please listen closely, I won't say it twice,
so try to remember this bit of advice.

If you want to enjoy those new shoes on your feet,
WATCH OUT FOR THE CARS WHEN YOU'RE
CROSSING THE STREET!

Name:_____

Let's Summarize

Directions: Below are the first five stanzas of the poem "Watch Out!" Use the signal words as sentence starters to summarize what happened first, next, then, and last.

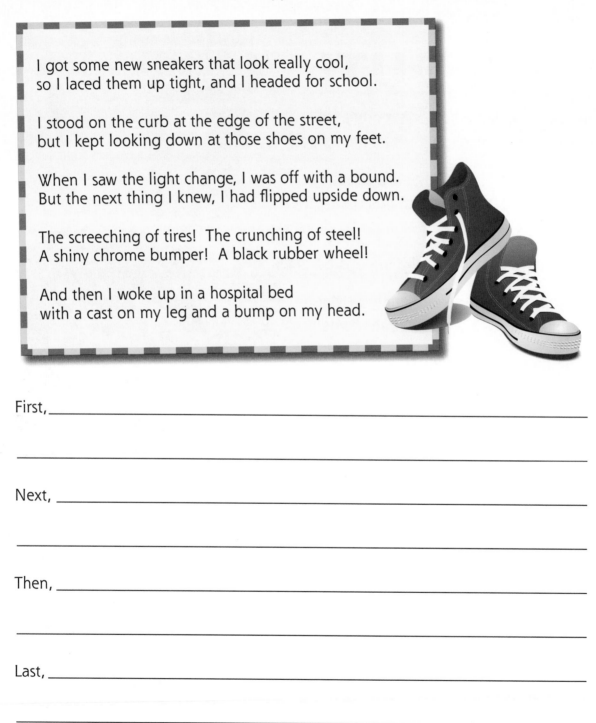

I got some new sneakers that look really cool,
so I laced them up tight, and I headed for school.

I stood on the curb at the edge of the street,
but I kept looking down at those shoes on my feet.

When I saw the light change, I was off with a bound.
But the next thing I knew, I had flipped upside down.

The screeching of tires! The crunching of steel!
A shiny chrome bumper! A black rubber wheel!

And then I woke up in a hospital bed
with a cast on my leg and a bump on my head.

First,_____

_____

Next, _____

_____

Then, _____

_____

Last, _____

_____

Name: _____

Watch Out

Below are five words that are small but powerful. They are used to make phrases that tell us such things as how, when, where, and why.

in	with	on	of	for

Directions: Fill in the correct missing word in each of the boxed phrases below.

1. I laced them up tight, and I headed _____ **school**.

2. I stood _____ **the curb** at the edge _____ **the street**.

3. When I saw the light change, I was off _____ **a bound**.

4. The screeching _____ **tires**! The crunching _____ **steel**!

5. Then I woke up _____ **a hospital bed** _____ **a cast** on my leg.

6. Enjoy those new shoes _____ **your feet**.

7. Watch out _____ **the cars** when you're crossing the street!

Extension

The little words that introduce phrases can make a big difference in meaning. Prove it. Write a different sentence using each of these phrases: *in the car, with the car, on the car, of the car,* and *for the car.*

The Colors of Childhood

In this next letter to Mr. Witherspoon, Paul Shapiro admits to being reckless, but thinks that it is not a problem because he wants to be a movie stuntman. Mr. Witherspoon writes a poem about childhood stunts—"The Colors of Childhood."

Making Connections

- Prepare students to draw parallels from their own lives with what they will read. Ask students if they have ever accidentally injured themselves. Ask students to think about what they were doing and tell whether it was their own fault it happened, or if it happened for some other reason. Give students time to reflect and then call on several students to share their experiences.

- Tell students that they will listen as you read the letter from Paul and the poem Mr. Witherspoon wrote for him. Afterward, ask students what Mr. Witherspoon meant by saying that the colors of childhood are black and blue.

Comprehension Strategy: Comparing Characters

- Distribute copies of the letter and poem or display them for the class.

- Ask students to describe what Paul is like (*reckless, daring, careless, inattentive, self-confident*). Then tell students to think back to the previous poem about Laura—the girl with the broken leg. Ask students to compare Paul and Laura. How are they alike and different? Invite several students to share their ideas.

Standards-Based Skill Focus: Compound Words

- Have students find and highlight the word *stuntman* in the letter. Tell students that *stuntman* is a compound word formed by putting together the nouns *stunt* and *man*.

- Ask students to speculate if the word *reckless* is a compound word or not, and why. After a few students share their thoughts, explain that *reckless* is not a compound word. Remind students that a compound word is made up of two words that can stand alone, and when combined they keep their original meanings.

- Distribute copies of page 60 and have students complete the activity independently.

Vocabulary Word Study

- Explain to students the importance of being able to use and spell words in order to consider them part of their working vocabularies.

- Distribute copies of page 61. Review the directions and have students complete the page on their own.

Dear Mr. Witherspoon,
    I am not a klutz, but I'm constantly hurting myself. My mother says it's my own fault for being so reckless, but how will I ever get to be a stuntman in the movies if I don't practice?
                                    Your friend,
                                    Paul Shapiro

The Colors of Childhood

I ran in my room,
bounced once on the bed,
did a flip in the air,
and fell right on my head.

On the seat of my bike
I stood straight and tall,
as I waved to my mom
and crashed into a wall.

The colors of childhood?
I think there are two.
The first one is black.
The other is blue.

Name:_____

Compounding

I. Directions: Create and write six compound words by combining words from List A with words from List B. Write your words on the lines.

List A			
bath	butter	cross	sun
day	door	down	ear
fighter	free	eye	sand
hand	moon	out	wood

List B			
light	fly	room	milk
lash	walk	road	time
ring	box	ball	way
down	side	knob	town
brow	shake		

_____ _____ _____

_____ _____ _____

II. Directions: Now use each of the compound words you made in a sentence.

1. _____

2. _____

3. _____

4. _____

5. _____

6. _____

Name: _____

The Colors of Childhood

Directions: Below is a copy of Paul's poem, "The Colors of Childhood." However, one word in each line is spelled incorrectly. Your job is to find and circle each misspelled word and write it correctly on the blank.

I ran in my rome, _____

bounced wants on the bed, _____

did a flipp in the air, _____

and fell rite on my head. _____

On the seet of my bike _____

I stood striaght and tall, _____

as I wavd to my mom _____

and crasht into a wall. _____

The colers of childhood? _____

I think there are too. _____

The frist one is black. _____

The other is bleu. _____

Extension

In his letter, Paul mentions his mother. From what he says, how do you think his mother reacts when Paul hurts himself?

The Moment of Truth

In his letter to Mr. Witherspoon, Stephen Newbury says that there is a bully in his neighborhood. However, Stephen has a reason for not being concerned. Mr. Witherspoon explains in the poem "The Moment of Truth."

Making Connections

- Prepare students to draw parallels from their own lives with what they will read. Ask students to reflect on the following questions: What is a bully? Have you ever encountered a bully? What should someone do about a bully? Give students time to discuss the questions with a partner or a small group. Then ask one person from each pair or group to share what the pair or group discussed.

- Tell students that they will listen as you read a letter from Stephen about a neighborhood bully and the poem Mr. Witherspoon wrote for him, "The Moment of Truth."

Comprehension Strategy: Clarifying

- Distribute copies of the letter and poem or display them for the class.

- Ask students to find each of the following phrases in the poem: *moment of truth, got up in my face*, and *yellow through and through*.

- Ask a volunteer to read the first phrase in context (i.e., the line or lines in which it appears). Then ask several students to clarify what the phrase might mean in that context. Repeat with the other phrases.

Standards-Based Skill Focus: Antonyms

- Ask students to identify two examples of opposites in the middle stanza (*big/small, strong/weak*). Remind students that words with opposite meanings are called *antonyms*.

- Have students find the words *scared* and *nothing* in the same stanza. Ask: Which would be an antonym of *scared—frightened* or *brave*? Which would be an antonym of *nothing—something* or *zero*?

- Distribute copies of page 64 and have students complete the skill activity independently.

Vocabulary Word Study

- Write the following commonly confused words on the board: *through, tough, though*, and *thorough*. Then point out their differences in pronunciation, spelling, and meaning. Challenge students to find any examples of these words in the poem.

- Distribute copies of page 65. Then have students complete the word study individually.

Dear Mr. Witherspoon,

There's a bully in my neighborhood. He's twice as big as I am, but I'm not scared of him because I can run twice as fast as he can.

Your friend,
Stephen Newbury

The Moment of Truth

My world was once a wonderful place
until Bradley the bully got up in my face.
He said, "You're yellow through and through!"
Now what was I supposed to do?

He's big! I'm small!
He makes me feel like I'm nothing at all.
He's strong! I'm weak!
I'm standing here too scared to speak.

This bully's twice as big as me,
So should I fight? Or should I flee?
I guess I'll do what must be done...
RUN! RUN! RUN! RUN!

Name:_____

Just the Opposite

Directions: Rewrite each sentence below so that it means just the opposite. Do this by changing only the bold word.

1. I went to pour the cereal and the box was **full**! _____

_____

2. I was **glad** that the big game was rained out. _____

_____

3. We had a **terrible** time at the party. _____

_____

4. Tim scored the **least** points of all. _____

_____

5. The dog ate **none** of its food last night. _____

_____

6. Mom **frowned** when she opened the box. _____

_____

Name: _____

The Moment of Truth

Directions: One word is missing from each sentence below. It is a word from this list of commonly confused words. Write the correct word in each blank.

through	tough	though	thorough

1. We hiked _____ the woods.

2. That was a _____ test!

3. I did a _____ job cleaning my room.

4. I kept going, even _____ I was tired.

5. The tunnel went _____ the mountain.

6. They did a _____ search for the lost key.

7. _____ time ran out, she didn't stop.

8. Bullies think that they are so _____.

9. I thought that I'd never get _____ those math problems!

Extension

Why do you think bullies act the way they do? What do you think is the best way to handle a bully? Write your opinions and ideas.

Sticks and Stones

The next letter to Mr. Witherspoon is from Sylvia Marie Sanchez. She thinks that sometimes words are more hurtful than actual pain. Mr. Witherspoon understands and provides the poem "Sticks and Stones."

Making Connections

- Prepare students to draw parallels from their own lives with what they will read. Ask by a show of hands who has ever heard the saying, "Sticks and stones may break my bones, but words will never hurt me?" Discuss the meaning of this saying.

- Ask students to think of a time when words were used to hurt someone. Give students time to reflect. Then rather than asking them to share, ask for another show of hands to the question "Have you ever said something that you wished you could take back?"

- Tell students that they will listen as you read the letter from Sylvia about words that hurt and the poem Mr. Witherspoon wrote for her, "Sticks and Stones."

Comprehension Strategy: Questioning

- Distribute copies of the letter and poem or display them for the class.

- Reread the first stanza and then ask, "Why do you think Sylvia said mean things to her friend? Why do you think her friend answered by claiming that she never liked her anyway? Did Sylvia later regret what she said? How do you know? The poem doesn't tell us, but what do you think happened next?"

Standards-Based Skill Focus: Understanding Idioms

- Write the following idioms on the board: *heart of stone* and *break a heart*. Explain that these phrases are not about the actual heart—the organ in the chest—but about feelings. Ask students what the phrases really mean.

- Challenge students to think of other *heart* expressions they have seen or heard.

- Distribute copies of page 68 and have students complete the skill activity.

Vocabulary Word Study

- Emphasize to students the importance of understanding how words are related.

- Distribute copies of page 69. Give students a set time to complete the page individually. Do not reveal the answer to Part II (the words are all verbs/action words) until the time is up.

Dear Mr. Witherspoon,
  They say, "Sticks and stones can break my bones, but words can never hurt me." But I think words can hurt a lot, sometimes more than sticks and stones.
      Your friend,
    Sylvia Marie Sanchez

Sticks and Stones

I frowned and said, "You're such a bore.
You're not my best friend anymore."
"Then leave," she said. "Why should you stay?
I never liked you anyway."

I made my heart as hard as stone
and left her standing all alone,
but now I feel so sad and blue...
I wonder if she's lonely too.

They say that words can't hurt you,
but words have torn us apart.
Sticks and stones may break your bones,
but words can break your heart.

Name:_____

Heart-y Expressions

Directions: The poem "Sticks and Stones" is about how mean words can break someone's heart. The phrase *break someone's heart* does not mean what the words say. It is just an expression that means "hurt someone's feelings." There are many expressions that use the word *heart*. Read the list of meanings below. Then read each sentence. Next to each sentence, write the expression that shows what the "heart" expression really means.

changed his mind	is kind	be jealous	memorize
without hesitating	means well	be uncaring	saddened me

1. Grandma has a heart of gold. _____

2. He seems to have a heart of stone. _____

3. We had to learn the words by heart. _____

4. Dad had a change of heart. _____

5. I'd do that in a heartbeat. _____

6. I told my sister to eat her heart out. _____

7. The news made my heart sink. _____

8. Mom has her heart in the right place. _____

Name:_____

Sticks and Stones

I. **Directions:** One word is missing from each sentence below. It is a word from the poem "Sticks and Stones." Fill in the correct missing word.

wonder	break	said	frowned	hurt	standing	leave

1. I was sad and bored. I _____ and sighed.

2. I didn't want to be there, so I decided to _____ early.

3. I looked at my friend and _____, "This is such a bore."

4. It was mean, but I left my friend _____ there alone.

5. I began to _____ if she was mad at me for that.

6. Maybe not, but I'm sure that I _____ her feelings.

7. To lose her as my best friend would _____ my heart.

• •

II. **Directions:** Look again at all the words you filled in. Think about how they are related. Here's a clue: It has to do with what job they do in sentences. Write below what all these words have in common.

_____ .

Extension

In "Sticks and Stones" you learned about expressions. Here is an expression about words that you might have heard: *Actions speak louder than words.* What do you think this means? Explain and give an example.

Stuffed

In his letter to Mr. Witherspoon, Henry T. Hollis confesses that, when it comes to pizza, he turns into a pig. Mr. Witherspoon's poem "Stuffed" is a humorous look at not wanting to share a good thing and the consequence of that choice.

Making Connections

- Prepare students to draw parallels from their own lives with what they will read. Ask students to think of a food that they enjoy so much that they sometimes overeat to the point of being stuffed. Give students time to reflect and then call on various students to share their thoughts and ideas.

- Tell students that they will listen as you read the letter from Henry and the poem Mr. Witherspoon wrote for him, "Stuffed."

Comprehension Strategy: Genre—Rhythm & Rhyme

- Distribute copies of the letter and poem or display them for the class.

- Ask students if a poem is more like a paragraph or a song, and why. If no one suggests it, point out that, like a song, poems often have rhythm and rhyme.

- Have students first identify the rhyming pattern of "Stuffed." Demonstrate how to clap out the rhythm of the first stanza. Then have students clap out the rhythm of the remaining stanzas as they read them aloud.

Standards-Based Skill Focus: Fluency—Choral Reading

- Explain to students that fluent readers not only understand what they read but can read with expression and at an appropriate pace.

- Distribute copies of page 72.

- Divide the class into four numbered groups. Explain that everyone (E) will read the first two lines of each stanza in unison. Then, just the members of group 1 (G1) will read the second two lines of the first stanza. Group 2 (G2) will read the second two lines of the second stanza, and so on.

- After they have practiced, have the class perform the poem for an audience such as their parents, the principal, or another class.

Vocabulary Word Study

- Distribute copies of page 73.

- Remind students of the activity in which they identified the rhythm of the poem. Explain that now they are to think of six foods that have two syllables, or beats, and then use the pattern of the poem "Stuffed" to create their own poem using a food word to replace *pizza* in each blank.

Dear Mr. Witherspoon,

I've been learning to share and sometimes I'm pretty good at it; but when it comes to pizza, I turn into a big greedy pig.

Your friend,
Henry T. Hollis

STUFFED

Pizza! Pizza! Yes-sir-ee!
Pizza! Pizza! All for me!
Pepperoni! Mushroom too!
Not a single slice for you!

Hurry! Hurry! I can't wait!
Put that pizza on my plate!
Yes! Oh, yes! Oh, yes it's true!
All for me and none for you!

I eat. I eat. I cannot stop.
I fill my belly to the top,
but still I chew and chew and chew,
I will not stop to share with you.

Too stuffed to breathe...too stuffed to talk...
too stuffed to stand...too stuffed to walk...
I'm stuck forever in this chair.
WON'T SOMEONE TEACH ME HOW TO SHARE?

Name:_____

We're "Stuffed"

Directions: You will be participating in a choral reading of the poem "Stuffed." First, circle your assigned parts listed below. You will have the opportunity to practice your parts with the group. You do not have to memorize your part, but you should read it with expression and at the right pace. When the group is ready, you will be asked to perform "Stuffed."

E = Everyone   **G1 = Group 1**   **G2 = Group 2**

G3 = Group 3   **G4 = Group 4**

(E)   Pizza! Pizza! Yes-sir-ee!
Pizza! Pizza! All for me!

(G1)   Pepperoni! Mushroom too!
Not a single slice for you!

(E)   Hurry! Hurry! I can't wait!
Put that pizza on my plate!

(G2)   Yes! Oh, yes! Oh, yes it's true!
All for me and none for you!

(E)   I eat. I eat. I cannot stop.
I fill my belly to the top,

(G3)   but still I chew and chew and chew,
I will not stop to share with you.

(E)   Too stuffed to breathe...too stuffed to talk...
too stuffed to stand...too stuffed to walk...

(G4)   I'm stuck forever in this chair...
WON'T SOMONE TEACH ME HOW TO SHARE!

Name:_____

Stuffed

I. **Directions:** The poem "Stuffed" is about pizza. *Pizza* is a two-syllable word. On the lines below, write six more two-syllable words that name foods.

_____   _____   _____

_____   _____   _____

• •

II. **Directions:** Create your own poem in the style of "Stuffed." All you need to do is replace the word *pizza* with another two-syllable food word.

> Stuffed, Too
>
> _____! _____! Yes-sir-ee!
>
> _____! _____! All for me!
>
> Hurry! Hurry! I can't wait!
>
> Put that _____ on my plate!
>
> Yes! Oh, yes! Oh, yes it's true!
>
> All for me and none for you!

Extension

Illustrate your poem "Stuffed, Too."

A Perfect Puppy

The next letter to Mr. Witherspoon is from Amanda Orizaga. She loves her new puppy but not the mess the puppy makes. Mr. Witherspoon sympathizes and provides the poem "A Perfect Puppy."

Making Connections

- Prepare students to draw parallels from their own lives with what they will read. Ask, "Why do people get pets?" Give students time to share their ideas.

- Then say, "Whether you have a pet or not, take a moment to think of two reasons for having a pet and two reasons for not having a pet." Call on several volunteers to offer their reasons.

- Tell students they will listen as you read a letter from Amanda about her new pet and the poem Mr. Witherspoon wrote for her, "A Perfect Puppy."

Comprehension Strategy: Recognizing Alliteration

- Distribute copies of the letter and poem or display them for the class.

- Reread the first stanza aloud, purposely emphasizing the repeated use of the *p* sound. Explain that using the same beginning sound in most or many of the words in a phrase is called *alliteration*.

- Ask students if they know any tongue-twisters. After two or three are suggested, challenge students to create their own tongue-twisters. Then have them trade with a partner and try to say it five times fast.

Standards-Based Skill Focus: Double-Consonant Patterns

- Have students find and highlight all the words they can find in the poem that have double consonants (*puppy, cuddly, little, really*).

- Distribute copies of page 76. Have students work alone or in pairs to complete the skill activity.

Vocabulary Word Study

- Review the term *alliteration*. Explain that to be an alliteration, the same consonant sound must be repeated at the beginning of several words in a phrase or line.

- Write these phrases on the board and have students identify which is an example of alliteration: *a little lost lizard*; *a small, missing reptile*.

- Distribute copies of page 77. After students complete the activity, invite several volunteers to read aloud some of the phrases they created.

Dear Mr. Witherspoon,
   My daddy got me a puppy,
and I named her Princess.
And I really love her, but she's
a total mess. Some of the
things she does are so gross I
can't even tell you.
                    Your friend,
                    Amanda Orizaga

A Perfect PUPPY

My puppy seemed so perfect,
so cuddly and sweet,
with perfect little puppy eyes
and perfect puppy feet.

My puppy seemed so perfect,
but it wasn't really true.
My perfect little puppy
just made pee-pee in my shoe.

Name:_____

Seeing Double

I. Directions: Read each clue. Look at the part of the answer that is given. Figure out what the word is and then supply the missing part—a double consonant.

1. glad, cheerful: h a __ __ y

2. over filled: s t u __ __ e d

3. very thin: s k i __ __ y

4. jumping: h o __ __ i n g

5. used with nails: h a __ __ e r

6. a close friend: b u __ __ y

7. eat in tiny bites: n i __ __ l e

8. laugh quietly: g i __ __ l e

9. fuzzy foot coverings: s l i __ __ e r s

10. 1,000,000: m i __ __ i o n

11. bad, awful: h o __ __ i b l e

12. go fast: h u __ __ y

13. squirm: w i __ __ l e

14. baby cat: k i __ __ e n

15. juicy, red fruit: a __ __ l e

16. something learned: l e __ __ o n

II. Directions: Use the consonants *f, d, r, z,* or *n* to complete the words below.

1. This is my toy. He is a stu __ __ ed bear named Te __ __ y.

2. He is fu __ __ y, with fu __ __ y ears and a fu __ __ y grin.

Name: _____

A Perfect Puppy

Directions: Create phrases with alliteration. Supply one more word to each phrase that begins with the same sound as the other words. You may choose words from the list below or come up with your own.

Example: _____perfect_____ puppy paws

two	wiggly	parade	creatures
mouse	little	scaly	

1. _____ snakeskin

2. lucky _____ leprechaun

3. creepy, crawly _____

4. _____ tiny ticks

5. miniature _____ meal

6. proud peacock _____

7. wonderfully _____ worms

Extension

Amanda named her perfect puppy Princess. Use alliteration to name these imaginary pets: a daring dinosaur, a lazy lion, a talking toucan, a grumbling groundhog, and a feisty fish.

Bad Unicorns

While Amanda wrote about her real pet puppy, Heather Page O'Callaghan dreams of having a unicorn for a pet. Mr. Witherspoon considers that a bad idea and tells why in the poem "Bad Unicorns."

Making Connections

- Prepare students to draw parallels from their own lives with what they will read. Have students reflect on the pros and cons of having pets. Ask students to think about what makes a good pet and what makes a bad pet. Then ask a few students to suggest types of good pets and bad pets. Finally, ask students what they think would be their dream pet and why.

- Tell students that they will listen as you read a letter from Heather about her dream pet and the poem Mr. Witherspoon wrote for her, "Bad Unicorns."

Comprehension Strategy: Genre—Fantasy

- Distribute copies of the letter and poem or display them for the class.

- Reread the poem "A Perfect Puppy" (page 75). Point out that in Amanda's poem, Mr. Witherspoon wrote about something that could really happen, but in Heather's poem he told a story that was entirely make-believe. Tell students that a story with imaginary beings doing things that could never really happen is a *fantasy*.

- Challenge students to identify other stories they know or have read that would be classified as fantasy, and explain their reasoning.

Standards-Based Skill Focus: Parts of Speech—Noun/Verb

- Review the terms *noun* and *verb*: A noun is a naming word; A verb is an action word.

- Have students point to each of the following words in the first stanza and identify it as a noun (naming word) or verb (action word): *walked, morning, surprise, saw, unicorn,* and *mischief.* If necessary, point out that besides naming people, places, and things, nouns also name ideas, feelings (*surprise*), and conditions (*mischief*).

- Distribute copies of page 80. Have students work individually to complete the skill activity.

Vocabulary Word Study

- Have students find and highlight the following words in the poem: *mischief, trampling, poke, canoe, spoil, horrible,* and *pests.* Clarify meanings as needed.

- Distribute copies of page 81 and have students use the clues to complete the puzzle. Depending on your students' needs, you may decide whether to allow them to refer to the poem for help as they complete the puzzle.

Bad Unicorns

I walked outside this morning,
and much to my surprise
I saw a real-live unicorn
with mischief in his eyes.

He was trampling our garden,
so I told him he should stop,
but he ate my mother's rosebush
from the bottom to the top.

And then I screamed—OH NO!
WHAT AN AWFUL THING TO DO!
as he used his horn to poke a hole
in Daddy's new canoe.

I don't want to spoil your fun.
I don't want to make you sad.
But I learned today that unicorns
are really, really bad.

Some people think roaches are horrible.
Some people say rats are a curse.
But of all the pests that ever lived,
the unicorn's the worst.

Dear Mr. Witherspoon,
I think a unicorn would be a wonderful pet. If I had one, it would make me happy forever.
Your friend,
Heather Page O'Callaghan

Name:_____

Naming and Doing

Directions: You know that nouns are naming words and verbs are action words. Below are the last four stanzas from the poem "Bad Unicorns." Decide if each bold word is a noun or a verb. Then write it in the correct column.

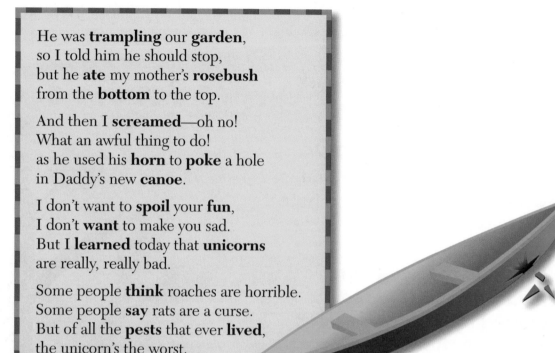

He was **trampling** our **garden**,
so I told him he should stop,
but he **ate** my mother's **rosebush**
from the **bottom** to the top.

And then I **screamed**—oh no!
What an awful thing to do!
as he used his **horn** to **poke** a hole
in Daddy's new **canoe**.

I don't want to **spoil** your **fun**,
I don't **want** to make you sad.
But I **learned** today that **unicorns**
are really, really bad.

Some people **think** roaches are horrible.
Some people **say** rats are a curse.
But of all the **pests** that ever **lived**,
the unicorn's the worst.

Nouns	Verbs

Name: _____

Bad Unicorns

Directions: Each answer is a word found in the poem "Bad Unicorns." Use the clues to figure out the mystery word.

1. a horse-like creature with a single horn: __ __ __ __ __ __ __
   ⭐

2. naughty behavior; trouble: __ __ __ __ __ __ __ __
   ⭐

3. beetle-like household pests: __ __ __ __ __ __
   ⭐

4. walking over and causing damage: __ __ __ __ __ __ __ __ __ __ __
   ⭐

5. harm; destroy; ruin: __ __ __ __ __
   ⭐

6. a light, narrow boat pointed at the ends: __ __ __ __ __
   ⭐

7. terrible; horrible; very bad: __ __ __ __ __
   ⭐

8. someone or something that is annoying or destructive: __ __ __ __
   ⭐

9. very unpleasant; nasty; horrifying: __ __ __ __ __ __ __
   ⭐

10. stick or push into; make a hole in: __ __ __ __
    ⭐

11. bone-like object on the heads of some animals: __ __ __ __
    ⭐

Extension

Use the starred letter from each word you filled in to spell the answer to this riddle:

Where is the only place unicorns exist?

___ ___ ___ ___ ___ ___ ___ ___ ___ ___ ___

A Dog's Life

The pet theme continues as Marcus writes to Mr. Witherspoon. However, the tone turns serious and reflective with Mr. Witherspoon's poem "A Dog's Life."

Making Connections

- Prepare students to draw parallels from their own lives with what they will read.

- Ask by a show of hands who has ever wondered about what a pet or another animal thinks about. Of those who raise their hands, ask a few to tell what the animal was doing at the time. Ask students if they have ever wished they were animals. Encourage volunteers to answer and explain why.

- Tell students that they will listen as you read a letter from Marcus who thinks dogs may be happier than people. Mr. Witherspoon tries to explain why dogs may be happier in his poem "A Dog's Life."

Comprehension Strategy: Mood and Tone

- Distribute copies of the letter and poem or display them for the class.

- Ask students to compare how Marcus views his pet dog to how his classmate Amanda (see page 75) views her pet puppy, Princess.

- Write the following words on the board: *serious, silly, thoughtful, resentful, joyous, troubled, light hearted,* and *deep*. Addressing one term at a time, ask students if the word does or does not describe the mood and tone of Marcus and his poem, and why.

Standards-Based Skill Focus: Final Punctuation

- Write the following sentences on the board: *I am happy. Are you happy? Wow! That's great!* Use them to review the three forms of final punctuation—period, question mark, and exclamation mark—and the function of each.

- Distribute copies of page 84 for students to complete individually.

Vocabulary Word Study

- Explain to students that although context clues, word association, etc. are all helpful, sometimes the only way to get the meaning of a word is to look it up in a dictionary.

- Distribute copies of page 85. First, students write the meaning of the term as they understand it in their own words. Then, they find out and mark if they were right or wrong by supplying evidence from a dictionary. If you desire, have students work in pairs to complete the activity.

A Dog's Life

My cocker spaniel, Rusty,
is a very happy dude.
All he does is lie around
and wait to get his food.

His life is free of problems.
The only thing he fears
is that someday I might forget
to scratch behind his ears.

My life is tests and homework,
a pressure pot of tension.
Sometimes it's like I'm living
in perpetual detention.

I'd never want to be a snake.
I'd never be a frog.
But lately I've been thinkin'
I might like to be a dog.

Dear Mr. Witherspoon,
My dog has such an easy life. All he ever does is sleep and eat and wait for me to scratch him. No fair!
Your friend,
Marcus Boorman

Name:_____

Straight from the Dog

Directions: The poem "A Dog's Life" is about a boy who thinks that his dog Rusty has it easy because he has nothing to be concerned about. Below is how Rusty might respond—if he could talk! Your job is to supply the correct final punctuation (.), (?), or (!) so that the sentences are statements, questions, or exclamations.

My name is Rusty ( ) My owner Marcus thinks that my life is free of problems ( ) He thinks that all I do is lie around and wait to get food ( ) Whoa ( ) Do you think that it is easy being a dog ( ) It's NOT ( ) I have plenty of things to worry about ( ) For example, I may look like I am lying around, but I am really on guard ( ) How else could I detect any little sound of danger if I wasn't holding still and listening very carefully ( ) Hey, the people don't pay attention ( ) They are always busy with things ( ) In fact, they depend on me to alert them by barking if something is out of the ordinary ( ) So, Marcus thinks he'd like to be a dog ( ) He can't even hear his alarm clock ( ) I'd like to see him try to do what I do ( ) Wouldn't you ( )

Name: _____

A Dog's Life

Directions: Each word below was used in Marcus's letter or the poem Mr. Witherspoon wrote for him, "A Dog's Life." First, write in your own words what you think it means. Then use a dictionary to check yourself. Write the evidence you found in the dictionary to support or correct your answer.

1. **dude**: I think it means _____

   I was _____ right _____ wrong. Evidence from the dictionary: _____

   _____

2. **tension**: I think it means _____

   I was _____ right _____ wrong. Evidence from the dictionary: _____

   _____

3. **perpetual**: I think it means _____

   I was _____ right _____ wrong. Evidence from the dictionary: _____

   _____

4. **detention**: I think it means _____

   I was _____ right _____ wrong. Evidence from the dictionary: _____

   _____

Extension

Do you think Marcus is right or wrong in thinking that dogs are free of problems and therefore happier than people? State your position and support it with reasons and details.

Phantom Fear

In his letter, David doesn't understand how he can be afraid of ghosts when he knows they don't exist. Mr. Witherspoon explains, but not before giving readers some chills in his poem "Phantom Fear."

Making Connections

- Prepare students to draw parallels from their own lives with what they will read. Discuss times when students have felt afraid of something even though they knew it was not real. Let a few students share their experiences.

- Ask students to consider and share their ideas about why being afraid of the dark is such a common thing, not just for children, but even for many adults.

- Tell students that they will listen as you read a letter from David, who knows there is no such thing as ghosts but is still afraid. Mr. Witherspoon expresses this fear in "Phantom Fear."

Comprehension Strategy: Imagery

- Distribute copies of the letter and poem or display them for the class.

- Direct students to close their eyes as you reread the first stanza. Ask several students what they "see" from the words in the poem.

- Have students find and underline the phrase *frosty breath of frozen fright*. Explain that instead of just saying *ghost*, carefully chosen descriptive words create vivid images in the minds of the readers. Have students find examples of imagery in the rest of the poem.

Standards-Based Skill Focus: Descriptive Adjectives

- Draw the outline of a ghost on the board. Write the word *ghosts* inside the shape. Challenge students to come up with words that could describe ghosts, and write these on lines coming out from the shape.

- Distribute copies of page 88.

- Remind students that words that describe nouns are called *adjectives*. Point out that the activity page contains descriptive lines from the poem "Phantom Fear." Direct students to fill in the descriptive adjectives for the given nouns and then, at the bottom, draw the images that come into their minds when reading their vivid descriptions.

- Encourage students to share their answers with partners.

Vocabulary Word Study

- Have students find and highlight the following words in the poem: *specters, frosty, prowlers, howlers, ease, combination,* and *imagination*.

- Distribute copies of page 89. Invite students to use these words to solve the puzzle.

PHANTOM FEAR

Dear Mr. Witherspoon,
    I'm afraid of ghosts. I know there's no such thing as a real ghost, but things don't have to be real to be scary. A make-believe ghost is just as scary as a real one.
                                Your friend,
                                David Verderame

When I am in my bed at night
I always need to have a light.
Without it, there would be no way
for me to keep the ghosts away.

Kooky-spooky-screechy-specters!
Stinky-clinky-chain-collectors!
Frosty breath of frozen fright
haunting houses every night.

My daddy says they aren't real,
which doesn't change the way I feel,
'cause in the dark, when I can't see,
they seem as real as real can be.

Sneaky-creaky-peeky-prowlers!
Tiny-shiny-whiny-howlers!
Floating fluffs of smoky gray
hiding at the edge of day.

Deep down I know my dad is right,
but knowing doesn't ease the fright.
I guess it's quite a combination—
darkness and imagination!

There are no ghosts beneath my bed,
what scares me most is in my head.
It's really strange! How can it be?
The thing I fear the most is ME!

Name:_____

Describing Ghosts

I. **Directions:** Supply the missing descriptive adjectives in the following lines from the poem "Phantom Fear."

_____ - _____ - _____ specters!

_____ - _____ - _____ collectors!

_____ breath of _____ fright

haunting houses every night.

_____ - _____ - _____ prowlers!

_____ - _____ - _____ howlers!

_____ fluffs of _____ gray

hiding at the edge of day.

• •

II. **Directions:** Draw in detail what you imagine as you read these descriptions.

Name:_____

Phantom Fear

Directions: Use the clues to solve the puzzle. The answers are words in David's poem.

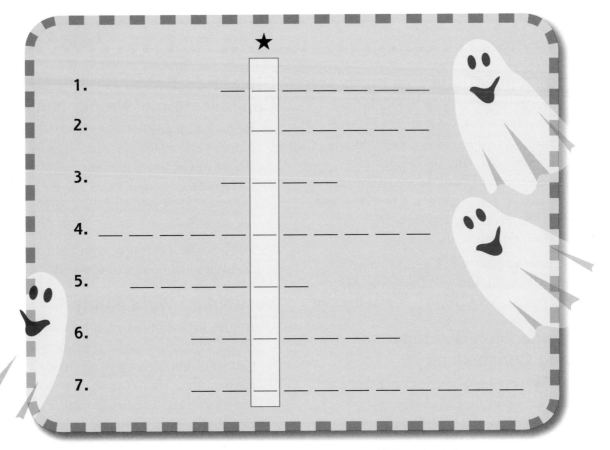

1. a ghostly image or vision

2. something that hollers, shrieks or yowls

3. relieve, lessen, or make better

4. the mind's ability to create images and ideas

5. icy cold and white

6. intruder; someone moving about in secret looking to steal or rob

7. the mixture of different things into one

Extension

Use the letters in the column under the star to spell the answer to this riddle:
What word names something that isn't really there?

____ ____ ____ ____ ____ ____ ____

Dressing Up

The next letter to Mr. Witherspoon is from Kaitlin Verderame. She wants a poem that expresses how she feels when she is in her Halloween costume. Mr. Witherspoon responds with the poem "Dressing Up."

Making Connections

- Prepare students to draw parallels from their own lives with what they will read. Ask students to speculate about why people enjoy dressing up in costumes. Then ask them to think of a costume they have worn or seen that was a favorite, and why. Call on various students to share their thoughts and experiences.

- Tell students they will listen as you read a letter from Kaitlin and the poem Mr. Witherspoon wrote for her, "Dressing Up."

Comprehension Strategy: Drawing Conclusions

- Distribute copies of the letter and poem or display them for the class.

- Explain that good readers recognize information directly stated in the text, but also have to draw conclusions based on information not directly stated. Ask students: What costume you think Kaitlin was wearing and what clues led them to that conclusion? Does Kaitlin enjoy dressing up? How do you know? Does Kaitlin wear the same costume every year? How can you tell? Accept all reasonable answers that can be supported.

Standards-Based Skill Focus: Capitalization of Proper Nouns

- Begin by having students find the name of a holiday in the poem (Halloween) and what kind of letter it begins with (capital). Review that the names of holidays, months of the year, and days of the week are always capitalized.

- Have students complete the skill activity on individual copies of page 92.

Vocabulary Word Study

- Remind students of what they learned about alliteration—the repeating of the first sound in a group of words or a phrase. Explain that Mr. Witherspoon used this technique again in this poem.

- Have students highlight the following phrases in the poem: *yucky-yellow, gizzard-green,* and *graveyard-gray.*

- Distribute copies of page 93. Tell students that it is their turn to create fun-to-read phrases using alliteration. Review the directions together and then direct students to complete the activity on their own.

Dear Mr. Witherspoon,
When my mother introduces me to her friends, they usually say something like, "What a beautiful child!" But they wouldn't say that if they saw me on Halloween. On Halloween, I am one ugly creature.

Your friend,
Kaitlin Verderame

Dressing Up

My mother says I'm pretty
and my mother's always right,
but once a year I turn into
a very ugly sight.

My skin is yucky-yellow.
My hair is gizzard-green.
I wear a pair of vampire fangs
that make my face look mean.

My fingernails are long and curved.
My lips are graveyard-gray.
And little kids who see me
start to scream and run away.

At Halloween, I like to look
as scary as can be,
an ugly sight for just one night,
then POOF! I'm back to me.

Name: _____

Calendar Quest

I. **Directions:** Proper nouns name particular people, places, and things, and begin with capital letters. The names of the days of the week, months of the year, and special days such as holidays are proper nouns. Find and underline any word that should be capitalized below. Then write the word correctly on the line.

1. It's fun to trick-or-treat on halloween. _____

2. The word wednesday has a silent *d*. _____

3. The 4th of july is a night for fireworks. _____

4. Why is thanksgiving always on a thursday? _____

5. Where I live, january is the coldest month. _____

6. On saturday night, we are going out to dinner. _____

7. Who will be your valentine on february 14? _____

8. My uncle is coming to visit this christmas. _____

9. We get homework every day except fridays. _____

10. Easter can fall in march or april. _____

II. **Directions:** Everyone has only one birthday—the day you were born. Write the month, day, and year of your birthday.

_____

Name: _____

Dressing Up

Directions: Mr. Witherspoon uses alliteration in Kaitlin's poem as a fun way to describe the colors of her skin, hair, and lips in her ugly Halloween costume. Remember that alliteration is purposely repeating the same beginning sound in a group of words or phrase. Mr. Witherspoon used the phrases below to describe yellow, green, and gray. Now, you take over the task. Use alliteration to fill in a describing word for the rest of the colors.

yucky yellow	gizzard green	graveyard gray

1. _____ blue

2. _____ red

3. _____ orange

4. _____ purple

5. _____ black

6. _____ brown

7. _____ pink

8. _____ white

Make a sketch of Kaitlin in her costume as described in the poem "Dressing Up."

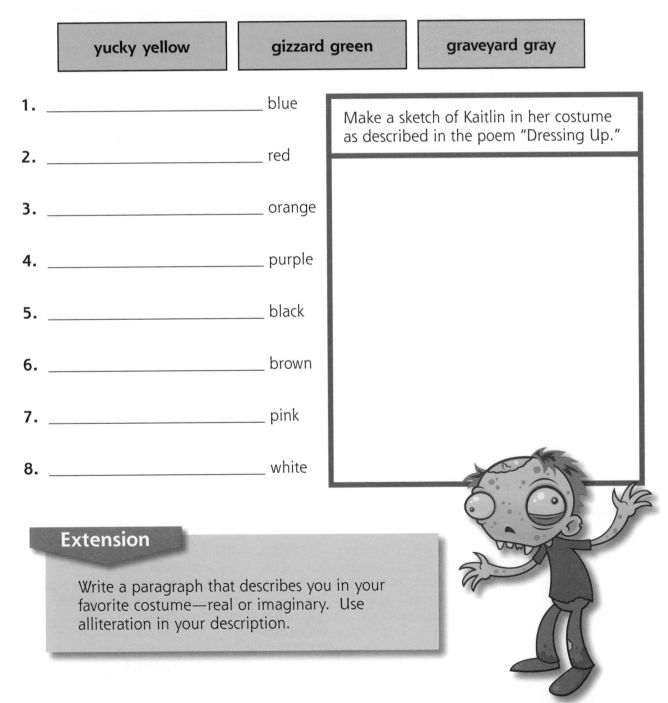

Extension

Write a paragraph that describes you in your favorite costume—real or imaginary. Use alliteration in your description.

A Thanksgiving Cheer

The holiday theme continues as Phil Martin writes that he likes Thanksgiving but feels sorry for the turkey. Mr. Witherspoon's "A Thanksgiving Cheer" takes a twist on something to be thankful for.

Making Connections

- Prepare students to draw parallels from their own lives with what they will read. Ask students to think about how their families celebrate Thanksgiving. Give students time to reflect and then call on various volunteers to describe their family traditions. (Some students may not have traditional family celebrations; therefore, only ask those students who volunteer.)

- Tell students they will listen as you read a letter from Phil and the poem Mr. Witherspoon wrote for him, "A Thanksgiving Cheer."

Comprehension Strategy: Main Idea

- Distribute copies of the letter and poem or display them for the class.

- Challenge students to summarize the poem in a single sentence. Allow several students to share their attempts. Write a few of these on the board.

- Ask the group to come up with a consensus sentence that best summarizes the main idea of the poem. It could be one on the board or a new one that combines elements of those mentioned. Example: There is much to be thankful for on Thanksgiving, but most of all we should be thankful that we are not the turkey.

Standards-Based Skill Focus: Fluency—Read and Refrain

- Use the read-and-refrain activity on page 96 for fluency practice—reading with appropriate expression, volume, tone, and pace.

- A refrain couplet needs to be added after each stanza of the original poem. Have students copy the refrain on each pair of lines. Example:

  Table's all set, let's take our place!
  I can't wait to stuff my face!

- Divide the class into four numbered groups. Explain that Group 1 (G1) reads the first three lines, and then everyone reads the Refrain in unison. Group 2 (G2) reads the next three lines, followed by everyone reading the Refrain, and so on. Allow students to practice several times.

Vocabulary Word Study

- Distribute copies of page 97.

- Have students use a light colored marker or crayon to highlight the words as they find them.

Dear Mr. Witherspoon,
I like Thanksgiving
dinner, but I feel sorry
for the turkey.
Your friend,
Phil Martin

A Thanksgiving Cheer

Sweet potato pie!
Sweet potato pie!
Mama's gonna bake some
sweet potato pie!

Cranberry sauce!
Cranberry sauce!
Mama's gonna make some
cranberry sauce!

Turkey in the oven!
Turkey in the oven!
Mama's got a big fat
turkey in the oven.

Thanks is the word!
Thanks is the word?
THANKS I WAS NOT
BORN A BIRD!

Name:_____

Read and Refrain

Directions: A refrain is a part of a poem (or song) that is repeated at the end of each verse. First, after each verse, copy the refrain your teacher has chosen. Next, circle your assigned parts on the parts list below. Be ready to practice and read with expression, not too loud or soft, and at the right speed.

G1 = Group 1	G2 = Group 2	G3 = Group 3	G4 = Group 4	Refrain = Everyone

(G1)   Sweet potato pie!
        Sweet potato pie!
        Mama's gonna bake some sweet potato pie!

(Refrain)   _____

        _____

(G2)   Cranberry sauce!
        Cranberry sauce!
        Mama's gonna make some cranberry sauce!

(Refrain)   _____

        _____

(G3)   Turkey in the oven!
        Turkey in the oven!
        Mama's got a big fat turkey in the oven!

(Refrain)   _____

        _____

(G4)   Thanks is the word!
        Thanks is the word?
        Thanks I was not born a bird!

(Refrain)   _____

        _____

Name: _____

A Thanksgiving Cheer

Directions: Phil's poem is about Thanksgiving—a holiday usually celebrated with a feast of different foods. The list in the word box includes foods that were served at the first Thanksgiving as well as those traditionally served today. Find each food word in the puzzle. Look up ↑, down ↓, and diagonally ↗↖↙↘.

Food Word List

turkey
potatoes
squash
dressing
beans
beets
gravy
onions
honey
carrots
stuffing
pumpkins
cranberries
pie
bread
nuts
sauce

A	W	E	C	R	T	Y	U	I	I	O	P
S	D	C	R	H	F	G	B	G	N	M	Q
P	O	T	A	T	O	E	S	R	T	A	S
U	B	Q	N	R	D	N	B	A	T	H	A
M	E	R	B	G	R	W	E	V	P	T	U
P	A	Z	E	A	C	O	E	Y	R	U	C
K	N	P	R	A	N	U	T	S	F	R	E
I	S	X	R	P	D	E	S	S	V	K	E
N	S	P	I	E	S	D	U	O	T	E	D
K	L	F	E	A	Q	D	J	N	G	Y	C
S	W	V	S	T	U	F	F	I	N	G	R
M	H	E	R	T	A	F	U	O	B	Y	F
J	S	D	R	E	S	S	I	N	G	H	V
A	Z	X	W	Z	H	Q	M	S	N	N	Q

Extension

Make a list of 10 foods you would like to have served for a Thanksgiving feast.

Nature's Tiny Building Blocks

The next letter from Dennis Dannel is the first of several that are science related. For Dennis's poem, Mr. Witherspoon explains that everything is made up of atoms.

Making Connections

- Prepare students to draw parallels from their own lives with what they will read. In pairs, ask students to each name several objects. Then ask students to categorize the objects they named into solids, liquids, or gases. Tell students that even though they named different objects, the objects are all made up of the same things.

- Encourage students to listen for the answer to what all things are made of as you read the poem "Nature's Tiny Building Blocks."

Comprehension Strategy: Genre—Poetic License

- Distribute copies of the letter and poem or display them for the class.

- Write the term *poetic license* on the board. Explain that there are many rules for writing, such as capitalization, punctuation, sentence structure, and the correct use of words. These rules apply to writing stories, paragraphs, letters, and almost everything else, with one exception—poetry. When writing a poem, an author may use poetic license. Poetic license means that poets have a license to disobey the standard rules of writing.

- Challenge students to study Mr. Witherspoon's poem to look for examples of poetic license.

Standards-Based Skill Focus: Coordinating Conjunctions

- Write the words *and, for, nor, but, or, yet,* and *so* on the board. Tell students these words are coordinating conjunctions and are used to connect portions of sentences.

- Ask students to find the word *and* in the poem. Have students identify what is being connected in the sentence.

- Distribute copies of page 100. Do the activity together as a group, or have students complete the page individually.

Vocabulary Word Study

- Write the words *air* and *fair* on the board. Ask students if these words rhyme.

- Add the word *everywhere* to the board. Ask students if this word rhymes with *air* and *fair*. Ask students if the spelling pattern is the same as in the first two words. Tell students that rhyming words do not have to have the same spelling pattern in order to rhyme.

- Distribute copies of page 101. Have students complete the activity on their own.

Nature's Tiny Building Blocks

Hear us shout! Hear us sing!
We atoms are in everything!

In a liquid? In a gas?
Even in a solid mass?

YES!
Hear us shout! Hear us sing!
We atoms are in everything!

In every little grain of sand?
In every single foreign land?

YES!
Hear us shout! Hear us sing!
We atoms are in everything!

In my water? In my air?
Atoms in my underwear?

YES!
Even in your shoes and socks,
we're nature's tiny building blocks.
So hear us shout, and hear us sing—
ATOMS MAKE UP EVERYTHING!

Dear Mr. Witherspoon,
My big sister says that atoms are like tiny building blocks and that everything in the whole world is made out of atoms. I think it's probably true, but it seems a little hard to believe.
Your friend,
Dennis Dannel

Name:_____

Coordinate Those Conjunctions

Directions: Circle the coordinating conjunctions in the sentences below. Then write what is being connected on the line below each sentence.

and	but	or	yet	for	nor	so

1. Do you want pie or ice cream for dessert?

   _____

2. She wanted to do well on the test, so she studied hard.

   _____

3. Jose ordered a hamburger and French fries for dinner.

   _____

4. Mom likes to watch neither football nor basketball on TV.

   _____

5. I wanted to buy a popsicle but did not have enough money.

   _____

6. We were sweating after recess, for it was a very hot day.

   _____

Name: _____

Nature's Tiny Building Blocks

Directions: Below is part of the poem "Nature's Tiny Building Blocks." Find the words that rhyme in the poem and write them on the lines. Check yes if the rhyming words have the same spelling pattern. Check *no* if the rhyming words have different spelling patterns.

Nature's Tiny Building Blocks

Hear us shout! Hear us sing!

We atoms are in everything!

_____ Yes ☐ No ☐

_____

In a liquid? In a gas?

Even in a solid mass?

_____ Yes ☐ No ☐

_____

In every little grain of sand?

In every single foreign land?

_____ Yes ☐ No ☐

_____

In my water? In my air?

Atoms in my underwear?

_____ Yes ☐ No ☐

_____

Extension

Think of other pairs of words that rhyme. Tell if the spelling pattern is the same or different.

A Birthday Wish

In the next letter to Mr. Witherspoon, Melissa Hofstadtler wonders why people are afraid of snakes—except her. Mr. Witherspoon answers with the poem "A Birthday Wish."

Making Connections

- Prepare students to draw parallels from their own lives with what they will read. Ask by a show of hands who is afraid of snakes. Then call on several students to tell why they think many people are afraid of snakes.

- Ask students what they know about snakes. Write responses on the board in a column labeled "What We Know." Ask students what they would want to know about snakes before they would hold one. Record their responses in a second column labeled "What We Want to Know."

- Tell students that they will listen as you read a letter from Melissa about snakes and the poem Mr. Witherspoon wrote for her, "A Birthday Wish."

Comprehension Strategy: KWLS Organizer

- Tell students that a good way to analyze text is to organize information in a graphic organizer, such as the KWLS. Review the information you recorded in the first two columns.

- After reading the poem, create a third column labeled "What We Learned" and ask students for input to write in that column.

- Label a fourth column "What We Still Want to Know." Ask students what they still want to know about the character. Record their responses on the chart.

Standards-Based Skill Focus: Homophones—There, Their, They're

- Write the words *there*, *their*, and *they're* on the board. Ask students how they are alike and different. Explain that words that sound the same but that have different meanings and spellings are called *homophones*.

- Have students complete the skill activity on individual copies of page 104 to practice using these common homophones correctly.

Vocabulary Word Study

- Explain to students that one useful tool for understanding and learning vocabulary is a thesaurus—a tool that lists synonyms (words that mean the same) and antonyms (words that mean the opposite). If possible, demonstrate using a printed thesaurus or the thesaurus function on a computer word-processing program.

- Distribute copies of page 105. Review the directions together and have students work in pairs to complete the activity.

A Birthday Wish

I know they don't have legs or wings,
but snakes are still my favorite things.
Now please don't scream and make a fuss,
'cause snakes are really scared of us.

We're so big, and they're so small,
that's why they fear us most of all,
and if you see one, night or day,
that snake will try to crawl away.

Their skin is dry and smooth and sleek.
They eat one tiny meal a week.
And snakes will seldom make a mess
'cause they make potty even less.

I like dogs, and I like fish,
but this year for my birthday wish,
I want ice cream! I want cake!
But most of all I WANT A SNAKE!

Dear Mr. Witherspoon,
    A lady came to our school,
and she told us all about snakes.
She even had a snake, and I
was the only one who wasn't
afraid to pet it.

                Your friend,
                Melissa Hofstadtler

Name:_____

There, Their, and They're

Directions: Study the meanings of the homophones below. Then write the correct word in each blank of the story.

there	their	they're

Slim and Slither

Bob and Joey live next door. _____ my best friends. I go to

_____ house after school. I go _____

because my mom works and _____ mom is home. I like to go

_____ because _____ fun to hang around with.

I especially like _____ pets. They have two snakes. It's okay.

_____ little and harmless. _____ names are Slim

and Slither. We take them out of _____ cages and play with them.

Once I asked my mom if I could bring Slim and Slither over to our house. She said,

"_____ better off next door. They belong

_____." I think she wants them to stay

_____ because she's just scared. I'll teach

my mom about snakes and why _____

nothing to be afraid of. Do you think that will change her mind?

Name: _____

A Birthday Wish

Directions: *Synonyms* are words that mean the same or almost the same. *Antonyms* are opposites. Each word in the left column is a word from the poem "A Birthday Wish." Write a synonym and an antonym for each word. Use a thesaurus if you need help. Then answer the questions below the chart.

Word	Synonym	Antonym
fuss		
scared		
fear		
dry		
smooth		
sleek		
tiny		
seldom		

1. If someone puts up a fuss, did he object or agree? _____

2. Would something sleek feel smooth or harsh? _____

3. Should you brush your teeth seldom or frequently? _____

Extension

Make a KWLS chart about another animal. Use books, encyclopedias, or websites to find out more about the animal and to fill in the "L" (What I Learned) section of the chart.

A Compost Lesson

In the next letter to Mr. Witherspoon, Jennifer Cloud is disgusted by a demonstration her teacher puts on. Mr. Witherspoon responds with the poem "A Compost Lesson."

Making Connections

- Prepare students to draw parallels from their own lives with what they will read. Elicit students' prior knowledge about worms by posing these questions and encouraging discussion of their answers: What do you know about worms? Who has seen a worm? How does it look? Who has held a worm? How does it feel? Where do worms live, and what do they eat?

- Tell students they will listen as you read a letter from Jennifer about a demonstration her teacher gave involving worms and the poem Mr. Witherspoon wrote for her, "A Compost Lesson."

Comprehension Strategy: Guess and Verify

- Explain to students that there is a difference between what they think and what they know.

- Write the word *garbage* on the board and ask students what they think it means. Accept all responses without indicating if they are accurate.

- Tell students that you are going to verify their responses by checking its meaning in a dictionary. Read the definition and ask students if it really means what they thought it meant. If necessary, clarify by comparing the meaning of *garbage* with that of *trash*. Repeat this process with the words *fertilizer* and *compost*.

Standards-Based Skill Focus: Changing Tense

- Begin by reviewing that present tense means that the action is happening now, or in the present, and past tense means that the action happened before, or in the past.

- Explain that, when telling a story, it is important to make sure that the tense is correct. Is the action happening now, or did it already happen?

- Distribute copies of page 108.

- Depending on your students' needs, you may want to complete the page together as a group, or have students complete it in pairs or individually.

Vocabulary Word Study

- Write *blue/shoe* and *hood/mood* on the board. Ask which pairs rhyme. Explain that rhyming words can be tricky. Poets like Mr. Witherspoon know that rhyme has to do with sound, not spelling.

- Distribute copies of page 109. Challenge students to supply words that rhyme, including words that may not have the same spellings for the sounds.

Dear Mr. Witherspoon,
My teacher showed us how worms eat garbage and make fertilizer. It was one of the most disgusting things I've ever seen.

Your friend,
Jennifer Cloud

A Compost Lesson

My teacher got a bunch of food
that was old and beginning to spoil.
She put it in a plastic box
and mixed it up with soil.

And then she added worms!
(I promise this is true.)
She said we'd learn a lesson
when we saw what they would do.

First they wiggled just a little.
Then they all began to crawl.
Then they started eating rotten stuff
until they ate it all.

They ate a pile of garbage
that would make your stomach squirm.
So what did we all learn today?
BE GLAD YOU'RE NOT A WORM!

Name:_____

Changing Tense

Directions: Each word on the chart below appeared in the poem "A Compost Lesson." It is shown in the tense that was used in the poem. Fill in the other tense. The first one is done for you as an example. The word *came* was used in the past tense. In the present tense, the word is *come*.

Present Tense	Past Tense
learn	
	saw
promise	
	began
is	
	ate
	added
	wiggled
	mixed
	did
squirm	
	started
crawl	
	put

Name: _____

A Compost Lesson

I. **Directions:** Imagine that, like Mr. Witherspoon, you are planning to write a poem. Think of and write one or more words that rhyme with each word below. Remember, rhyming is about sound, not spelling!

1. mood _____

2. socks _____

3. hood _____

4. germs _____

5. wait _____

6. gotten _____

7. burn _____

8. firm _____

9. crust _____

10. shoe _____

11. all _____

12. I'll _____

II. **Directions:** Ready to try poetry? Complete these lines with your own words.

I watched them eat the garbage. It made my stomach squirm.

The most disgusting thing to be would have to be a _____

It's pretty gross to think about the things they do all day,

chomping down on rotten stuff while I go out and _____

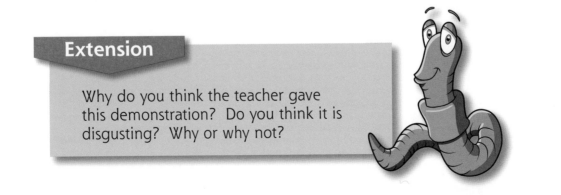

Extension

Why do you think the teacher gave this demonstration? Do you think it is disgusting? Why or why not?

Bug Body Armor

The next letter to Mr. Witherspoon is from Billy Tuttle, who thinks bugs are cool. Mr. Witherspoon understands and provides the poem "Bug Body Armor."

Making Connections

- Prepare students to draw parallels from their own lives with what they will read. Pose this question: Do all animals have bones? Allow students to respond to the question and to one another before telling them that some animals do not have bones—instead they have shells or other types of hard coverings on the outsides of their bodies. Challenge students to give some examples of these kinds of animals.

- Tell students that they will listen as you read a letter from Billy (who simply thinks bugs are cool) and Mr. Witherspoon's poem that tells us more about them, "Bug Body Armor."

Comprehension Strategy: Deconstructing Terms

- Distribute copies of the letter and poem or display them for the class.

- Begin by deconstructing the term *exoskeleton*. Explain that *skeleton* is a word meaning the hard framework that supports and protects the bodies of people and animals. The prefix, or word part added to the beginning, is *exo-*. This means "outside" or "external." If we put the two meanings together, we can figure out that *exoskeleton* means a hard framework that supports and protects the body and is on the outside.

- Remind students that good readers sometimes take apart words and look at smaller pieces to help figure out their meanings.

Standards-Based Skill Focus: Understanding Metaphor

- Review the meaning of *simile*—a comparison using *like* or *as*.

- Have students find examples of similes in the first stanza of the poem "Bug Body Armor" (*skin is hard as stone, shell as hard as armor plate*).

- Direct students' attention to the last line of the second stanza. Explain that here, rather than using *like* or *as*, the comparison is made directly—as if one thing actually were another thing, not just like it. It says an exoskeleton would make him into a human tank, not just look like one. Direct comparisons such as these are called *metaphors*.

- Distribute copies of page 112. Complete the skill activity together.

Vocabulary Word Study

- Write the following prefixes and their meanings on the board: *ex-* = out, *im-* = in. Then write the words *export* and *import*.

- Say, "Let's deconstruct these words. Both have a prefix added to *port*. *Port* means to carry. What do you think *export* means? *Import*?"

- Distribute copies of page 113 and have students complete it on their own.

Bug Body Armor

Bugs don't need a single bone
because their skin is hard as stone.
A shell as hard as armor plate
supports a bug's whole body weight.

Exoskeleton! Cool as can be!
I want a skin like that for me.
And then I'd have a bug to thank
for making me a human tank.

Name:_____

Making Metaphors

Directions: Imagine that you want to describe someone who moves slowly. You decide to compare him to a snail. One way is to use a *simile*—a comparison using *like* or *as*: *He is like a snail.* You could also use a *metaphor*—a direct comparison: *He is a snail.* Each description below is a simile. Reword it as a metaphor.

Example: (simile) I was so hungry that my stomach felt like an empty cave.
(metaphor) I was so hungry that my stomach was an empty cave.

1. My best friend and I are like two peas in a pod.

   _____

2. The ants were like an army invading the picnic.

   _____

3. Her long hair was as soft as silk flowing over her shoulders.

   _____

4. When it comes to sports, I am like an encyclopedia of facts.

   _____

5. An exoskeleton makes a bug like a miniature tank.

   _____

Name:_____

Bug Body Armor

Directions: One way to understand an unfamiliar word is to see if you can deconstruct it, or break it apart. Study the meanings of the word parts below. Then, for each numbered term, deconstruct it to figure out what it means. Write the meaning you figured out on the line.

Word Part	Meaning	Word Part	Meaning
bi-	two	port	carry
trans-	across	credit	believe
auto-	self	sect	cut
tele-	distant	graph	write
de-, dis-	opposite	scend	climb

Term   **Deconstructed Meaning**

1. transport _____

2. bisect _____

3. discredit _____

4. autograph _____

5. descend _____

6. teleport _____

Extension

Work with a partner to come up with as many words as you can that contain any of the word parts above.

The Big Circle

In the next letter to Mr. Witherspoon, Kiarah Beard turns the focus from animals to plants. Mr. Witherspoon uses personification to explain how plants start and end as seeds in the poem "The Big Circle."

Making Connections

- Prepare students to draw parallels from their own lives with what they will read. First, draw a circle on the board. Point out that it begins and ends at the same place. Explain that many things in nature follow a cycle—a series of events that repeat, beginning again where they just ended. Give the example of the water cycle.

- Ask students what else follows a repeating cycle. If no one suggests it, say "How about plants? They begin as seeds, grow, and make new seeds before they die."

- Tell students they will listen as you read a letter from Kiarah about seeds and the poem Mr. Witherspoon wrote, "The Big Circle."

Comprehension Strategy: Recognizing Personification

- Distribute copies of the letter and poem or display them for the class.

- Write the term *personification* on the board. Explain that this means giving plants, animals, or things human qualities, feelings, and words. In this poem, Mr. Witherspoon pretends that a seed can talk, feel, and act like a person. He writes the poem as if the seed wrote it—"I'm a seed that needs to grow."

- Challenge students to find examples of personification in the poems they have already studied or in other pieces of text.

Standards-Based Skill Focus: Subject/Verb Agreement—Is/Are

- Begin by reviewing singular and plural nouns. Identify the following nouns in the poem as singular (one) or plural (more than one): *roots*, *stem*, *leaves*, *bee*, and *flower*.

- Explain when to use *is* and when to use *are* in a sentence. If the subject noun is singular, use *is*. If the subject noun is plural, use *are*.

- Write the following on the board: one root is—but roots are; a stem is—but stems are; a leaf is—but leaves are; one bee is—but bees are; a flower is—but flowers are. Erase all the instances of *is* and *are*. Read these aloud again, but have students verbally supply the *is* or *are*.

- Distribute copies of page 116 for students to complete on their own.

Vocabulary Word Study

- Extend students' science content vocabulary. List on the board and discuss the following terms: *leaves*, *stem*, *fruit*, *roots*, *flower*, and *seeds*.

- Distribute copies of page 117. You may or may not want to leave the list of science words on the board for students' reference as they complete the activity.

Dear Mr. Witherspoon,

I liked learning about plants. I liked learning how plants start as a seed and go back to a seed at the end.

Your friend,
Kiarah Beard

The Big Circle

I'm a seed that needs to grow,
so hurry, sunshine, melt that snow.

My roots are creeping through the crud,
curling underneath the mud.

My stem is rising, long and green,
into the air so fresh and clean.

My luscious leaves are having fun,
basking in the morning sun.

Busy little buzzy bee,
I'm a flower, come to me.

I grew with such amazing speed,
but once again I'm just a seed.

Hurry, sunshine, melt that snow.
I'm a seed that wants to grow.

Name: _____

Is or Are?

Directions: Do you ever get confused about when to use *is* or *are*? First, look at the boldfaced subject of each sentence below. If the subject is singular, write *is* on the line. If the subject is plural, write *are* on the line.

I Am a Plant...

My **roots** _____ creeping through the crud. (is/are)

My **stem** _____ rising, long and green. (is/are)

My luscious **leaves** _____ having fun. (is/are)

My **flowers** _____ colorful and bright. (is/are)

A buzzy **bee** _____ landing on me. (is/are)

The **bees** _____ taking the pollen away. (is/are)

My **day** _____ happy and carefree. (is/are)

Seeds _____ going to grow from me. (is/are)

New **plants** _____ going to be popping up. (is/are)

The **sun** _____ going to shine on them, too. (is/are)

I hope **they** _____ as happy as me! (is/are)

Name:_____

The Big Circle

Directions: Answer each personified riddle below with the name of a part of a flowering plant or tree.

1. I am the part of a plant or tree that is underground. I absorb water and minerals for the plant. What am I? _____

2. I am the part of a flowering plant that carries water and minerals from the roots to the rest of the plant. I am sometimes called the stalk. What am I? _____

3. I am the flat green part of the plant that basks in the sun, but I am doing a big job—photosynthesis—using light to make food for the plant. What am I?

   _____

4. I am the most colorful part of a plant. I use my petals to attract bees and birds, which help me by carrying the pollen to where it needs to go to make more plants like me. What am I? _____

5. I am the part of the plant that contains the seeds. I am also the part that is a favorite food to many animals (and people) because I am often sweet and juicy. What am I? _____

6. I am the tiny part of a plant that contains everything needed to make a whole new plant. I am found in the fruit or flowers of plants and in the cones of some kinds of trees. What am I? _____

Extension

Make a diagram of a plant that shows all of the parts above. Be sure to label each part.

Morning, Noon, and Night

In this next letter to Mr. Witherspoon, Buck Ivon proudly proclaims that he knows how to tell time by watching the sun. Mr. Witherspoon sneaks in a little Earth science with his poem "Morning, Noon, and Night."

Making Connections

- Prepare students to draw parallels from their own lives with what they will read. Ask students to take a moment to think about the sun. Does it always appear in the same place in the sky? Where is it in the morning? Midday? Evening? Where is the sun at night? Give students time to reflect and then call on various volunteers to share their thoughts.

- Ask students this follow-up question: Does the sun move? Explain that the sun actually does not move; it only seems to move. What is moving is Earth.

- Tell students that they will listen as you read a letter from Buck and the poem Mr. Witherspoon wrote for him, "Morning, Noon, and Night."

Comprehension Strategy: Listening for Information

- Use this activity to test students' listening skills. Tell students that you are going to read the poem aloud again. This time they are to listen for information.

- Have students orally or on paper answer these questions: In which direction would you look to see the sun rise? Set? What part of the day is the sun directly overhead? What two things does the sun fill the world with?

Standards-Based Skill Focus: Sequence

- Begin with this challenge. Say, "I am thinking of a word that means the order in which things happen. Who can name the word?" If no one answers *sequence*, offer additional clues. (It begins with *s*. It rhymes with *cents*.) When someone answers correctly say, "Yes, *sequence* means the order that things happen."

- Have students chorally reread the first stanza of the poem. Write the words *First*, *Next*, and *Last* on the board. Ask students to identify the sequence of the three events described.

- Distribute copies of page 120 and have students complete the activities.

Vocabulary Word Study

- Remind students that a compound word is made up of two words that can stand alone, and, when combined, keep their original meanings.

- Have students identify the compound words in the poem (*sunshine*, *breakfast*, *midday*, and *overhead*).

- Distribute copies of page 121. Review the directions and then have students complete the page on their own.

Morning, Noon, and Night

Dear Mr. Witherspoon,

I learned how to tell what time it is by looking at the sun, so now I always know when it's time to eat.

Your friend,
Buck Ivon

Morning sunshine in the east—
Scrambled eggs! A breakfast feast!
Midday sunshine overhead—
Lunch today is pizza bread!
Golden sunshine in the west—
Time for supper! Turkey breast!

Sunshine, sunshine, oh so sweet.
Sunshine makes my life complete.
It fills my world with light and heat
and tells me when it's time to eat.

Name:_____

Order, Please

I. **Directions:** Read each group of events. Think about what order they should be in. Then, write numbers to show the correct sequence.

1. Put on your seat belt. Get in the car. Drive to the store.

☐   ☐   ☐

2. Brush your teeth. Go to bed. Turn out the light.

☐   ☐   ☐

3. Mail the note. Write a thank-you note. Receive a gift.

☐   ☐   ☐

II. **Directions:** Make a list of six things you did to get ready this morning. Write the list in the correct sequence.

1. _____

2. _____

3. _____

4. _____

5. _____

6. _____

Name: _____

Morning, Noon, and Night

Directions: Below is a copy of the first part of the poem "Morning, Noon, and Night." Fill in the missing words. Choose from the list of words below. Hint: Each of the correct missing words is a compound word.

morning	light	breakfast	noon	above
overhead	sky	midday	sunshine	special

Morning sunshine in the east—

Scrambled eggs! A _____ feast!

_____ sunshine _____—

Lunch today is pizza bread!

Golden _____ in the west—

Time for supper! Turkey breast!

Extension

Reread the poem above. Then, copy this statement and fill in the direction words that correctly complete it.

The sun rises in the _____ and sets in the _____.

No One to Blame but Me

In her letter to Mr. Witherspoon, Sarah Sobel takes responsibility for her own actions but isn't happy about it. Mr. Witherspoon responds with the poem "No One to Blame but Me."

Making Connections

- Prepare students to draw parallels from their own lives with what they will read. Ask students to reflect on something that they have all experienced—having to place blame where it belongs. Ask students to take a moment to think about a time when something went wrong and they had no one to blame but themselves. Give students time to share their thoughts or experiences in pairs.

- Tell students that they will listen as you read a letter from Sarah and the poem Mr. Witherspoon wrote for her, "No One to Blame but Me."

Comprehension Strategy: Drawing Conclusions

- Distribute copies of the letter and poem or display them for the class.

- Lead students in chorally rereading the poem. Then have students respond to these questions: What can you conclude about what kind of balloon is in the poem? What can you conclude about helium-filled balloons that is different from air-filled balloons? Can you conclude from the poem that the writer knew that cutting the string would cause the balloon to go to the ceiling? How?

Standards-Based Skill Focus: Indefinite Adjectives

- Review that *adjectives* are describing words. Ask what the adjective is in this sentence: I have one balloon. Explain that the adjective *one* tells an exact number. Then ask what the adjective is in this sentence: There are many balloons. Point out that the adjective *many* does not tell an exact number.

- Explain that adjectives that do not give a definite number or amount are called *indefinite adjectives*. Ask students for other possible examples (*all*, *each*, *many*).

- Distribute copies of page 124 and have students complete the skill activity.

Vocabulary Word Study

- Help students strengthen their vocabulary and spelling skills. Have students underline the following words in the poem: *ceiling*, *weighs*, and *scientific*.

- Point out that each word has either an *ie* or an *ei* in them. Give the "rule" *i* before *e* except after *c* or when the two letters make the long *a* sound. Ask how the rule applies to *ceiling* and *weighs*. Then clarify that the "rule" doesn't apply all the time. Some words, such as *scientific*, are exceptions.

- Distribute copies of page 125 for students to complete.

Dear Mr. Witherspoon,
        It's sad when bad things happen, but
it's even sadder when the bad things that
happen are your own fault. I don't like it
when I have no one to blame but myself.
                    Your friend,
                    Sarah Sobel

No One to Blame but Me

There it is, my blue balloon.
It's on the ceiling of my room.
Helium weighs less than air
and that is why it's stuck up there.

And yet these scientific laws
are not the one and only cause.
I need to add just one more thing—
it's up there 'cause I cut the string.

Name:_____

More or Less Indefinite

Directions: Indefinite adjectives usually answer the question of how many or how much without giving a definite or exact number or amount. Read each sentence below. Find and underline the indefinite adjective or adjectives.

all	any	each	every	few
many	some	most	several	

1. At the circus, the clown was carrying many balloons.

2. The balloons were in all different colors.

3. There were so many to choose from.

4. Most were round, but some were in different shapes.

5. Some had designs, and several were plain.

6. Every balloon was pretty.

7. I would have liked to have had any one of them.

8. A clown asked if we would like to buy some of his balloons.

9. We each looked at Dad.

10. Dad said, "I guess I could spare a few dollars."

11. We each picked out one.

12. It was hard to decide because there were several choices.

Name: _____

No One to Blame but Me

Directions: Two letters are missing from each word below—an e and an *i*—but in which order should they appear? Generally, *i* comes before e, except after c or when it makes the long *a sound*.

1. Helium w ___ ___ ghs less than air.

2. I find your story hard to bel ___ ___ ve.

3. Sometimes my n ___ ___ ghbors get noisy.

4. There was a spider crawling on the c ___ ___ ling.

5. Noah is my best fr ___ ___ nd.

6. Did you rec ___ ___ ve the invitation to my birthday party?

7. The game was cancelled because the f ___ ___ ld was too wet.

8. Be sure to call before ___ ___ ght o'clock tonight.

9. My aunt says that I am her favorite n ___ ___ ce.

10. Ten horses pulled the sl ___ ___ gh through the snow.

Extension

Spelling rules can be helpful, but you still need to know that many words don't follow the rules. These words are exceptions to the rule you learned for *ie/ei* above: *either*, *weird*, *seize*, and *neither*. You will just have to learn these by heart. Practice now by writing each word three times and then using it in a sentence.

Me! The Free!

Maria Sanchez writes that, although children are supposed to like puppet shows, she doesn't. With the poem "Me! The Free!" Mr. Witherspoon shows Maria that it's fine to like or not like whatever she chooses.

Making Connections

- Prepare students to draw parallels from their own lives with what they will read. Ask students to take a moment to think of something that they were supposed to like but did not. Call on various volunteers to share their thoughts or experiences.

- Tell students that they will listen as you read a letter from Maria and the poem Mr. Witherspoon wrote for her, "Me! The Free!"

Comprehension Strategy: Signal Words

- Distribute copies of the letter and poem or display them for the class.

- Write the following words on the board: *however*, *but*, *although*, *instead of*, and *on the other hand*. Explain that these signal to readers that a contrast or a change in direction is coming.

- Have student volunteers complete these sentence starters: I like chocolate, but _____; I may be small, however _____; Although I am just a kid, _____; Instead of going to school every day, _____; Sometimes I wish that I were grown-up, but on the other hand _____. Challenge students to identify the signal words and the contrast that follows.

Standards-Based Skill Focus: Double Negatives

- Write the following sentence on the board and challenge students to identify what is wrong with it: I don't like no kinds of cheese. Explain that the words *don't* and *no* are negatives, and as a rule, a sentence should never contain more than one negative.

- Demonstrate how to correct the sentence by changing the word *no* to *any*. Then continue with these examples: I haven't never seen a puppet show (change *never* to *ever*); I don't know nothing about them (change *nothing* to *anything*).

- Distribute copies of page 128 and have students complete the activity.

Vocabulary Word Study

- Give students an opportunity to use the words they know by sight and sound in writing.

- Distribute copies of page 129. As students do the activity, avoid helping them by supplying ideas or spellings. What students choose (and how they use and spell the words) will give you insight into their ability to accurately use the words in their speaking and writing.

Dear Mr. Witherspoon,
     Children are supposed to like puppet shows, but I don't. I think they're silly. Is something wrong with me?
                    Your friend,
                    Maria Sanchez

Me! The Free!

I like flowers, pink and blue.
I like playing peek-a-boo.
I like to read; I like to sing;
and dancing is my favorite thing.

Now listen, listen, listen, please.
I do not like the smell of cheese.
I don't like wearing fancy clothes.
I don't like silly puppet shows.

I'm not the boss, not yet, it's true;
big people tell me what to do.
But in my head I'm always free
'cause what I like is up to me.

So give me flowers, pink and blue,
and play a little peek-a-boo,
but keep that pile of fancy clothes,

AND STUFF THOSE PUPPETS
UP YOUR NOSE!

Name:_____

No, Nothing, Never

Directions: Each sentence below has a double negative. Rewrite it correctly.

1. I don't have no sisters.

I don't have _____ .

2. It wasn't never seen before.

It wasn't _____ .

3. He didn't have nothing left.

He didn't have _____ .

4. It wouldn't go no further.

It wouldn't go _____ .

Name: _____

Me! The Free!

Directions: The poem "Me! The Free!" is about making your own choices about what you like and do not like. Fill in the blanks below with your own choices.

What I Like Is up to Me

1. I like the colors _____ and_____,
but I don't much like the color _____.

2. A game I like to play is _____, but I don't really enjoy
playing _____.

3. Two foods I really like are _____ and _____.
However, I can't stand _____!

4. When it comes to music, I like _____, but I am not fond of
_____.

5. If I could go anywhere, I'd like to visit _____, but going to
_____ doesn't interest me.

6. When I grow up, I'd like to be _____, but I'd never like to be
_____.

Extension

Write your own poem about your likes and dislikes. You can use the pattern of the poem "Me! The Free!" or any other poem you have read.

Book Ends

In his letter to Mr. Witherspoon, Tyrone Byrd turns to the serious when he laments about coming to the end of a good story. With the poem "Book Ends," Mr. Witherspoon shows that he understands that feeling very well.

Making Connections

- Prepare students to draw parallels from their own lives with what they will read. Ask students to take a moment to think of a book or story that seemed so real that they felt like they were a part of the story or one that they enjoyed reading so much that they were sorry it came to an end. Allow time for students to talk in pairs or small groups.

- Tell students that they will listen as you read a letter from Tyrone and the poem Mr. Witherspoon wrote for him, "Book Ends."

Comprehension Strategy: Mood and Tone

- Distribute copies of the letter and poem or display them for the class.

- Explain that poems and other types of narrative writing convey moods. The tone of the writing is determined and expressed by the writer. Write several words on the board that show mood, such as *serious, angry, suspenseful, silly, anxious, affectionate, hopeful,* and *regretful.* Ask students to contribute more mood words for the list.

- Have students reread the poem and offer their ideas for what mood or tone Mr. Witherspoon tried to convey in his poem for Tyrone.

Standards-Based Skill Focus: Figurative Language

- Present and explain the terms *literal* and *figurative: literal*—the words mean exactly what is said; *figurative*—the words represent something other than what is said. Students will need several examples to understand this concept.

- Distribute copies of page 132. Use this as a teaching tool and work through the skill activity together.

Vocabulary Word Study

- Distribute copies of page 133.

- Read and review the meanings of the words on the page that show mood. Further develop students' understanding by randomly choosing a word and asking a volunteer to give a situation that could be described with that mood word. (Example: *anxious*—waiting for the bus when it is late.)

Dear Mr. Witherspoon,

I read my first chapter book and I liked it a lot, but at the end I felt sad. The guy the book was about seemed so real to me it was like I was losing a friend.

Your friend,
Tyrone Byrd

BOOK ENDS

I have lived each page of this book,
it made me laugh and cry,
but now I've come to the end
and it's time to say good-bye.

Yet my heart is still in the story,
and the hero is my friend.
Oh, I hope someday to come back this way
and read this book again.

Name:_____

Figuratively Speaking

Directions: Read each sentence. Decide if it means what the words actually say or means something other than what the words say. Write *literal* or *figurative*. Explain your answers.

1. We put our heads together to solve the problem. _____

_____

_____

2. Outside it was raining cats and dogs. _____

_____

_____

3. I didn't win. I guess that's the way the cookie crumbles. _____

_____

_____

4. Mom said to look both ways before crossing the street._____

_____

_____

5. All that money I earned was burning a hole in my pocket. _____

_____

Name: _____

Book Ends

Directions: Poems, like people, can have different moods. Each of the words below can be used to describe mood. Make sure you can read each word and that you understand its meaning. Then rewrite the list in alphabetical order.

joyous	affectionate	angry	playful
lonely	suspenseful	cranky	gloomy
hopeful	calm	excited	thoughtful
silly	regretful	anxious	serious

_____ _____

_____ _____

_____ _____

_____ _____

_____ _____

_____ _____

_____ _____

_____ _____

Extension

Pick three of Mr. Witherspoon's poems. Identify the mood of each.

Letter from Jonathan/Mr. Witherspoon's Response

In his letter, Jonathan writes to Mr. Witherspoon asking for a whole new set of poems.
Mr. Witherspoon responds, not with a poem, but by telling him no.

Making Connections

- Prepare students to draw parallels from their own lives with what they will read. Ask students to take a moment to think of a time when they asked for something and they did not get what they wanted. Call on various volunteers to share their thoughts or experiences.

- Tell students that they will listen as you read a letter from Jonathan. After you read the letter, ask students how they think Mr. Witherspoon will respond. Allow students to share and then read Mr. Witherspoon's response.

Comprehension Strategy: Character Development

- Distribute copies of the letter and Mr. Witherspoon's response or display them for the class.

- Explain that although these letters are not very long, they reveal something about both Jonathan and Mr. Witherspoon's characters. Refer back to the two original letters Mr. Witherspoon sent to Madison. Compare what Mr. Witherspoon said in those letters to what he said in the letter to Jonathan. What can we learn about Mr. Witherspoon from the tone in the letter he wrote back to Jonathan? Is it serious? Silly? Funny? How do you know? Allow time for discussion of the two letters.

Standards-Based Skill Focus: Applying Comprehension Strategies

- Tell students that authors can write for a variety of reasons: to entertain, to inform, and to ask a question.

- Have students think of the various reasons they write. Create a list of their ideas on the board.

- Distribute copies of page 136. Point out that Jonathan and Mr. Witherspoon have distinct purposes for writing their letters. Have students work with partners to discuss and write answers for the questions. Then review their responses as a group.

Vocabulary Word Study

- Write the name *Greer* on the board. Ask students to identify the beginning letter (*g*) and sound (/g/) in Jonathan's last name. Ask students if they can think of other sounds the letter *g* makes. If students do not think of it, tell them the letter *g* can also make the /j/ sound as in the name *George*.

- Distribute copies of page 137. Tell students they will explore the sounds of the letter *w* in the activity they complete today. Have them work independently to complete the page and then review it as a group.

Dear Mr. Witherspoon,

Madison McDonald told me you wrote poems for her whole class. She said they just sent you a bunch of notes about what they wanted their poems to be about, and you wrote them. That was really a good idea. So here are some notes from the kids in my class. Do you think you could write some poems for us? Please?

Your friend,
Jonathan Greer

Dear Mr. Greer,

Thank you for your wonderful letter. I'm very sorry, but I'm moving to Antarctica and will not be able to fulfill your request.

Sincerely,

Mr. Witherspoon

P.S.—There is no mail delivery at the South Pole.

Name: _____

What Do You Think?

Directions: Answer the questions below about Jonathan Greer's letter to Mr. Witherspoon and Mr. Witherspoon's reply.

1. Who is Jonathan Greer, and why did he write to Mr. Witherspoon?

_____

2. Do you think Jonathan expects Mr. Witherspoon to say yes? Why?

_____

3. Why does Mr. Witherspoon say that he's moving to Antarctica?

_____

4. Why do you think Mr. Witherspoon included the "P.S." at the end of his letter?

_____

Name:_____

Letter from Jonathan/Mr. Witherspoon's Response

I. Directions: The words in the box below are words from Jonathan's or Mr. Witherspoon's letters. Each word begins with the letter *w*, but there are three different beginning sounds made by these words. Sort the words by their beginning sounds and write them in the correct columns. Then add one more word of your own to each column.

| wrote | whole | wanted | will | wonderful |

Sounds like /w/	Sounds like /r/	Sounds like /h/

II. Directions: Use one word from each column in a sentence.

_____

_____

_____

Extension

Think of other letters that have multiple sounds. Write three words for each letter and sound you can think of.

Answer Key

Page 20

Part I

1. capital
2. comma

Part II

1. commas added after the greeting (Dear Mrs. McBride,) and the closing (Your student,)
2. commas added after the greeting (Dear Students,) and the closing (Yours truly,)

Page 21

Part I

can't, you've, that's, you're, it's, don't, I'm

Part II

contractions in this order: I'm, you're, can't, it's, don't

Page 24

Answers will vary.

Page 25

Part I

Circled: know, castle, would, knife, wrestle, talk, listen, watch, Lincoln, half, knee, answer, wrote, kneel, whole, could, often, knot, calf

Part II

Silent *l*: would, talk, Lincoln, half, could, calf

Silent *t*: castle, wrestle, listen, watch, often

Silent *k*: know, knife, knee, kneel, knot

Silent *w*: wrestle, answer, wrote

(Note: the *w* in *wh* is not considered silent)

Page 28

1. poem
2. Madison
3. Morgan
4. Morgan
5. secret
6. Madison
7. the class
8. Mr. Witherspoon

Page 29

3 **Across**—yesterday

4 **Across**—unfair

5 **Across**—perfect

1 **Down**—special

2 **Down**—written

6 **Down**—totally

Page 32

1. worked
2. getting
3. writing
4. kept
5. closing
6. sleeping
7. asked
8. walked

Page 33

1. sleeping
2. reading
3. thinking
4. trying
5. keeping
6. getting
7. finishing
8. closing

Page 36

1. noun
2. adjective
3. adjective
4. noun
5. noun
6. adjective
7. adjective
8. noun
9. noun
10. adjective

Page 37

Answers will vary, but must include at least three sensory words in each category.

Page 40

Part I

All words are one syllable except: Recess (2), favorite (3), around (2), outside (2), only (2), about (2), recess (2), and Bobby (2).

Part II

1. No. Proof will vary.
2. No. Proof will vary.

Page 41

Part I

Answers will vary, but must be two-syllable words.

Part II

Answers will vary, but must be two-syllable words.

Page 44

Part I

4 similies—as fast as a flash, as quick as a spark, run like a cheetah, swim like a shark.

Part II

Poems will vary.

Answer Key *(cont.)*

Page 45

1. conquer
2. capture
3. cheetah
4. rescue

Page 48

Quotation marks added as follows:

"Good Morning,"

"What's the matter?" "Why aren't you eating?"

"I can't. My tooth is so loose that I am afraid that I will swallow it." "What would happen if I swallow it, Dad?"

"Probably nothing," "But, maybe you should let me pull it out."

"No way!"

"Okay," "Just let me see how loose it is."

"You can look now, Dad,"

"Where is it?"

"That's for me to know and you to find out,"

Page 49

1. swollen
2. wimp, limp
3. splinter
4. cure
5. swallowed
6. wiggling

Page 52

1. does
2. don't
3. do
4. doesn't
5. does
6. don't
7. do
8. doesn't
9. do
10. doesn't

Page 53

Answers will vary, but must be words in the given families.

Page 56

Summaries will vary.

Page 57

1. for
2. on, of
3. with
4. of, of
5. in, with
6. on
7. for

Page 60

Part I

Answers will vary, but must be compound words made from words on the lists.

Part II

Answers will vary, but must be sentences using compound words.

Page 61

rome—room

wants—once

flipp—flip

rite—right

seet—seat

striaght—straight

wavd—waved

crasht—crashed

colers—colors

too—two

frist—first

bleu—blue

Page 64

Sentences may vary, but must be opposites. Suggested answers:

1. replace *full* with *empty*
2. replace *glad* with *mad*
3. replace *terrible* with *good*
4. replace *least* with *most*
5. replace *none* with *all*
6. replace *frowned* with *smiled*

Page 65

1. through
2. tough
3. thorough
4. though
5. through
6. thorough
7. Though
8. tough
9. through

Answer Key (cont.)

Page 68

1. is kind
2. be uncaring
3. memorize
4. changed his mind
5. without hesitating
6. be jealous
7. saddened me
8. means well

Page 69

Part I

1. frowned
2. leave
3. said
4. standing
5. wonder
6. hurt
7. break

Part II

They are verbs/action words.

Page 73

Part I

Answers will vary, but must be two-syllable food words.

Part II

Poems will vary, but must contain two-syllable food words.

Page 76

Part I

1. happy
2. stuffed
3. skinny
4. hopping
5. hammer
6. buddy
7. nibble
8. giggle
9. slippers
10. million
11. horrible
12. hurry
13. wiggle
14. kitten
15. apple
16. lesson

Part II

Answers may vary. Suggested: stuffed, Teddy, furry, fuzzy, funny

Page 77

Answers may vary. Suggested:

1. scaly snakeskin
2. lucky little leprechaun
3. creepy crawly creatures
4. two tiny ticks
5. miniature mouse meal
6. proud peacock parade
7. wonderfully wiggly worms

Page 80

Nouns: garden, rosebush, bottom, horn, canoe, fun, unicorns, pests

Verbs: trampling, ate, screamed, poke, spoil, want, learned, think, say, lived

Page 81

1. unicorn
2. mischief
3. roaches
4. trampling
5. spoil
6. canoe
7. awful
8. pest
9. horrible
10. poke
11. horn

Riddle answer: imagination

Page 84

Rusty (.) problems (.) food (.) Whoa (!) dog (?) **NOT** (!) about (./!) guard (.) carefully (?) attention (./!) things (.) ordinary (.) dog (./?) clock (./!) do (.) you (?)

Page 85

Answers will vary.

Page 88

Part I

Kooky-spooky-screechy

Stinky-clinky-chain

Frosty, frozen

Sneaky-creaky-peeky

Tiny-shiny-whiny

Floating, smoky

Part II

Drawings will vary.

Page 89

1. specter
2. howler
3. ease
4. imagination
5. frosty
6. prowler
7. combination

Riddle answer: phantom

Answer Key *(cont.)*

Page 92

Part I

1. Halloween
2. Wednesday
3. July
4. Thanksgiving, Thursday
5. January
6. Saturday
7. February
8. Christmas
9. Fridays
10. March, April

Part II

Students write their own birth date using correct capitalization.

Page 93

Answers will vary, but must be examples of alliteration.

Page 96

Refrain copied as directed.

Page 97

A	W	E	C	R	T	Y	U	I	I	O	P	
S	D	C	R	H	F	G	B	G	N	M	Q	
P	O	T	A	T	O	E	S	R	T	A	S	
U	B	Q	N	R	D	N	B	A	T	H	A	
M	E	R	B	G	R	W	E	V	P	T	U	
P	A	Z	E	A	C	O	E	Y	R	U	C	
K	N	P	R	A	N	U	T	S	F	R	E	
I	S	X	R	P	D	E	S	S	V	K	E	
N	S	P	I	E	S	D	U	O	T	E	D	
K	L	F	E	A	Q	D	J	N	G	Y	C	
S	W	V	S	T	U	F	F	I	N	G	R	
M	H	E	R	T	A	F	U	O	B	Y	F	
J	S	D	R	E	S	S	I	N	G	H	V	
A	Z	X	W	Z	H	Q	M	S	N	N	Q	

Page 100

1. or; pie/ice cream
2. so; do well on the test/studied hard
3. and; hamburger/French fries
4. nor; watch football/basketball
5. but; buy a popsicle/not enough money
6. for; sweating/hot day

Page 101

sing, everything—yes

gas, mass—no

sand, land—yes

air, underwear—no

Page 104

They're, their, there, their, there, they're, their, They're, Their, their, They're, there, there, they're

Page 105

Answers will vary, but must be synonyms and antonyms.

1. object
2. smooth
3. frequently

Page 108

Present Tense	Past Tense
learn	learned
see	saw
promise	promised
begin	began
is	was
eat	ate
add	added
wiggle	wiggled
mix	mixed
do	did
squirm	squirmed
start	started
crawl	crawled
put	put

Page 109

Part I

Answers will vary but must be rhyming words.

Part II

Answers may vary. Suggested: worm, play

Page 112

1. My best friend and I are two peas in a pod.
2. The ants were an army invading the picnic.
3. Her long hair was soft silk flowing over her shoulders.
4. When it comes to sports, I am an encyclopedia of facts.
5. An exoskeleton makes a bug a miniature tank.

Answer Key (cont.)

Page 113

Answers may vary. Suggested:

1. carry across
2. cut in two
3. opposite of believe
4. self-written (signature)
5. opposite of climb/go down
6. carry over a distance

Page 116

roots are, stem is, leaves are, flowers are, bee is, bees are, day is, Seeds are, plants are, sun is, they are

Page 117

1. roots
2. stem
3. leaves
4. flower
5. fruit
6. seed

Page 120

Part I

1. 2, 1, 3
2. 1, 2, 3 (or (1, 3, 2)
3. 3, 2, 1

Part II

Answers will vary but should be listed in order.

Page 121

breakfast

Midday, overhead

sunshine

Page 124

1. many
2. all
3. many
4. most, some
5. some, several
6. every
7. any
8. some
9. each
10. few
11. each
12. several

Page 125

1. weighs
2. believe
3. neighbors
4. ceiling
5. friend
6. receive
7. field
8. eight
9. niece
10. sleigh

Page 128

1. I don't have any sisters.
2. It wasn't ever seen before.
3. He didn't have anything left.
4. It wouldn't go any further.

Page 129

Answers will vary.

Page 132

1. Figurative
2. Figurative
3. Figurative
4. Literal
5. Figurative

Page 133

affectionate

angry

anxious

calm

cranky

excited

gloomy

hopeful

joyous

lonely

playful

regretful

serious

silly

suspenseful

thoughtful

Page 136

Answers will vary.

Page 137

Part I

Sounds like *w*: wanted, wonderful, will

Sounds like *r*: wrote

Sounds like *wh*: whole

Other answers will vary.

Part II

Answers will vary.

References Cited

Bottomley, D and J. Osborn. 1993. *Implementing reciprocal teaching with fourth- and fifth-grade students in content area reading*. ERIC document 361668.

Bromley, K. 2004. Rethinking vocabulary instruction. *The Language and Literacy Spectrum* 14: 3–12.

Carter, C. 1997. "Why reciprocal teaching?" *Educational Leadership* 54(6): 64–68.

Harris, T. and R. Hodges (Eds.). 1995. *The literacy dictionary: The vocabulary of reading and writing.* Newark, DE: International Reading Association.

Harvey, S. and A. Goudvis. 2000. *Strategies that work: Teaching comprehension to enhance understanding and engagement.* Portland, ME: Stenhouse Publishers.

Herrell, A., and M. Jordan. 2004. *Fifty strategies for teaching English language learners*. 2nd ed. Upper Saddle, NJ: Pearson Education, Inc.

Hosenfeld, C. 1993. *Activities and materials for implementing adapted versions of reciprocal teaching in beginning, intermediate, and advanced levels of instruction in English, Spanish, and French as a second/foreign language.* ERIC document ED370354.

Jensen, E. 1998. *Teaching with the brain in mind.* Alexandria, VA: Association for Supervision and Curriculum Development.

Keene, E. and S. Zimmermann. 1997. *Mosaic of thought.* Portsmouth, NH: Heinemann.

National Institute of Child Health and Human Development. 2000, Updated 2006. *Teaching children to read: An evidence-based assessment of the scientific research literature on reading and its implications for reading instruction.* Report of the National Reading Panel. Washington, D.C.: U.S. Government Print Office.

Pressley, M. 2001. Comprehension instruction: What makes sense now, what might make sense soon. *Reading Online.* 5(2): http://www.readingonline.org/articles/handbook/pressley/index.html

Rasinski, T.V. 2003. *The fluent reader.* New York, NY: Scholastic Professional Books.

Richek, M. 2005. Words are wonderful: Interactive, time-efficient strategies to teach meaning vocabulary. *The Reading Teacher.* 58(5): 414–423.

Rosenshine, B. and C. Meister. 1994. Reciprocal teaching: A review of the research. *Review of Educational Research.* 64(4): 479–530.

WIDA—housed within the Wisconsin Center for Education Research. 2007. English language proficiency standards. The Board of Regents of the University of Wisconsin System, http://www.wida.us/standards/elp.aspx

Contents of the CDs

Contents of the Teacher Resource CD

Poems and Activity Pages		
Lesson	Pages	Filename
1	19–21	lesson1.pdf
2	23–25	lesson2.pdf
3	27–29	lesson3.pdf
4	31–33	lesson4.pdf
5	35–37	lesson5.pdf
6	39–41	lesson6.pdf
7	43–45	lesson7.pdf
8	47–49	lesson8.pdf
9	51–53	lesson9.pdf
10	55–57	lesson10.pdf
11	59–61	lesson11.pdf
12	63–65	lesson12.pdf
13	67–69	lesson13.pdf
14	71–73	lesson14.pdf
15	75–77	lesson15.pdf
16	79–81	lesson16.pdf
17	83–85	lesson17.pdf
18	87–89	lesson18.pdf
19	91–93	lesson19.pdf
20	95–97	lesson20.pdf
21	99–101	lesson21.pdf
22	103–105	lesson22.pdf
23	107–109	lesson23.pdf
24	111–113	lesson24.pdf
25	115–117	lesson25.pdf
26	119–121	lesson26.pdf
27	123–125	lesson27.pdf
28	127–129	lesson28.pdf
29	131–133	lesson29.pdf
30	135–137	lesson30.pdf

Additional Resources	
Item	Filename
Page-turning Book	witherspoon.html
Instructional Plan	instructional.pdf
McREL Chart	mcrelchart.pdf
Activity Skill Corr. Chart	activitychart.pdf

Contents of the Audio CD

Track	Title
01	Madison's Request
02	Stuck
03	Madison's Reply
04	Mr. Witherspoon's Response
05	Pop!
06	The Recess Song
07	The One
08	The Cure
09	A Natural Bodily Function
10	Watch Out!
11	The Colors of Childhood
12	The Moment of Truth
13	Sticks and Stones
14	Stuffed
15	A Perfect Puppy
16	Bad Unicorns
17	A Dog's Life
18	Phantom Fear
19	Dressing Up
20	A Thanksgiving Cheer
21	Nature's Tiny Building Blocks
22	A Birthday Wish
23	A Compost Lesson
24	Bug Body Armor
25	The Big Circle
26	Morning, Noon, and Night
27	No One to Blame but Me
28	Me! The Free!
29	Book Ends
30	Letter from Jonathan/ Mr. Witherspoon's Response